VILLAIN

VILLAINS WE HAVE KNOWN

Reg Kray

arrow books

This edition published by Arrow Books Limited 1996

1 3 5 7 9 10 8 6 4 2

First published in the United Kingdom in 1993 by
N.K. Publications, Leeds.

Arrow Books Ltd
Random House UK Ltd, 20 Vauxhall Bridge Road, London SW1V 2SA

Random House Australia (Pty) Limited
20 Alfred Street, Milsons Point, Sydney,
New South Wales 2061, Australia

Random House New Zealand Limited
18 Poland Road, Glenfield
Auckland 10, New Zealand

Random House South Africa (Pty) Limited
PO Box 337, Bergvlei, South Africa

Random House UK Limited Reg No 954009

A CIP catalogue record for this book
is available from the British Library

Papers used by Random House UK Limited are natural, recyclable products
made from wood grown in sustainable forests. The manufacturing processes
conform to the environmental regulations of the country of origin.

ISBN 0 09 979781 X

Typeset by Deltatype Ltd, Ellesmere Port, Cheshire

Printed and bound in the United Kingdom by
Cox & Wyman Ltd, Reading, Berks

I dedicate this book to my brother Ron.
We walked the same path.

I wish to thank my friends Frank and Noelle Kurylo and Stephanie King, Helen Keating, Paul Marcus Henry and Leslie Joyce for encouragement given.

Contents

Villains on the Manors

The fact that London was made up of so many areas enabled villains to have what they called their own manor, a manor being another name for an area, and in whatever direction one would go, north, south, east or west, one could come across or encounter some of the villains I am about to mention. These villains were part of the London scene between the fifties and sixties, three that come to mind are Patsy Omara, Mike Connors and Chopper Watts.

Patsy was a hard-drinking villain who could be seen in the area of South London on most days but he would also frequent Soho and other areas of London. He was afraid of no one and enjoyed life to the full. At one time he, Freddie Foreman, my brothers Charlie, Ron and myself were in the one arm bandit machine business together. Patsy passed away at an early age just a few years ago.

If one was near Holborn Tube Station on any day of the week they would see a flower stall nearby and the person selling the flowers would be Mike Connors. He could not be mistaken, his face was a mass of razor cuts that had left deep scars. Mike had always been a villain and at one time had been attacked and cut badly outside White City Dog Track. He could always be seen at the big fights in the company of my friend Alex Steene and the late Jack Kid Burg who was exlightweight junior champion of the world. Mike was also a friend of mine like Patsy, but both are no longer with us.

Chopper Watts could be seen any day playing cards in the Stow Gambling Club in Walthamstow High Street. Chopper obviously got his reputation through the habit of carrying a chopper as a weapon. I found him to be a shrewd and likeable person. One time a firm from Upton Park went to the Stow Club looking for Chopper intending to do him injury but he escaped being hurt when he locked himself in the toilet and resisted all efforts to get him out. He was very lucky on this occasion because two of the firm were Teddy and Billy Robbins who came from Upton Park. As far as I know Chopper could be playing cards at the Stow Club today.

If one went east to Bethnal Green they might have seen the two local villains Willy and Johnny Collins who were brothers, chatting away whilst leaning on the railings just outside Bethnal Green Tube Station. At one time Willy was at a gambling club in the Aldgate area when he had an argument with Harry Lazar the ex-pro lightweight fighter. Willy knew that he would lose a fight with Lazar so he hit him over the head with a billiard cue; he said he did not need a referee. For many years amiable Johnny Collins visited Ron at Broadmoor. Ron was very upset when Johnny died a few years ago.

If we went north to the areas of Tottenham and Edmonton we would find Tommy Keys and his family. At one time Patsy Arragon had a feud with another villain. One day he went to the local barber shop down in Hoxton Market and sitting in the chair in front of him was his rival. Patsy took a razor from the shelf, opened it and slashed the fellow villain so badly that he needed one hundred stitches. After he came out of Dartmoor Prison Patsy opened a drinking club above a furniture shop in Tottenham High Street. I would go there regularly as Patsy was a good host and we got on well together. He had been given a seven-year sentence for the razor attack and served most of the sentence at Dartmoor Prison. I always found Patsy to be quite a likeable person and I hope that he is still alive and will read this chapter on him.

As we entered Edmonton we would be on Tommy Keys' manor. Tommy was the local villain and he and his family were always the local topic of conversation. Tommy's brother Barney, could play on a piano rock and roll and anything else better than anyone I knew. The Keys family were known for their fighting and hard-drinking times. Barney would often play the piano in the Double R Club which my brothers and I had on Bow Road in East London.

Anyone who travelled to the Senate Rooms Club at Highbury in North London would be met at the entrance by one of my favourite villains and oldest friends, Steve Murphy. He had the looks of a younger version of the ex-president of the United States, Ronald Reagan and he dressed just as good as him. Steve, like Patsy Arragon was a good club host and there was hardly any trouble on his premises. He was one of the top money getters of his day and has been brought up through the ranks of villainy with such people as Big Alf Melvin, Tommy Smithson and Tony Mulla so he had been in good company. Steve used to dress and look like a film star and to this day he still sends Ron and I Christmas cards.

If we looked around the Senate Rooms we might see Tommy Cowley sitting at the bar with a drink in his hand and chain-smoking while he chatted away to one of the club hostesses who would be sitting there with her legs crossed on the bar stool. Tommy was another friend of ours and was given a nine-month sentence for harbouring Frank Mitchell when he escaped from Dartmoor Prison. Tommy was slightly built and about five feet six in height, he had ginger hair and was a neat dresser. He was a compulsive gambler and practically lived in the speils which was another word for gambling clubs. Tommy had also done a four-year sentence at Maidstone Prison.

Perhaps we would drive over to the Queen's Public House on the corner of Upton Park. As we would enter we would see gathered at the bar the Upton Park Mob. They would all be there, our friends Jimmy and Georgie Woods, Porky and Dickie Bennett, Little Jacky Reynolds, Ted Machent, Ted and Billy Robbins and if it were a good night, the one and only Billy Hill. Everbody would be happy that Billy had joined them. Porky Bennett had just come out of serving seven years imprisonment down at Dartmoor. He had been convicted of razor slashing someone and for demanding money with menaces from Chinese restaurant owners in the dock area of Pennyfields in Chinatown. Porky would look immaculate with a single-breasted suit, waistcoat, white shirt and a dark tie and he would wear a smart trilby hat just as could be seen in a good gangster movie. Ted Robbins would be wearing a smart raincoat and a cloth check cap, George and Jimmy would be looking their usual immaculate selves and dangling from Jimmy's waistcoat would be a gold chain with a neat pocket watch. Both Jimmy and George would be wearing smart trilby hats. Little Jacky Reynolds would be sitting at one of the tables in the corner of the bar and one would notice that he had a jagged scar on the left-hand side of his face. His little alert brown eyes would be taking in all that he saw.

It was at this period of time that we had a gambling club at Wellington Way in Bow Road. Georgie Woods and Jacky Reynolds along with Limehouse Willie ran the gambling club for Charlie, Ron and myself. One day at the club Jacky Reynolds had a verbal argument with one of the Osbourne family from Bethnal Green. It was Buster Osbourne who had been a successful pro fighter at welterweight. I was in the club that day and noticed the argument which was going on. It lasted about a minute when I saw Jacky walk away and sit down at a table with Sammy Josephs. Sammy had done a ten-year sentence in Dartmoor for his part in the London Airport robbery of gold bullion that George and Jimmy Woods were also convicted of. I watched and saw Jacky get up from the table and go to the fireplace in the centre of the room where the coal fire was burning fiercely. I saw Jacky pick up the poker that was lying on the side of the fire and he placed it deep into the burning coals. He returned to the table and sat back with his friend Sammy Josephs. Buster Osbourne, like Jacky, was also a friend of mine so I went over to the table where Jacky was sitting and asked him what the problem was with Buster. He said they were arguing over a game of cards and that he would show the bastard if he wanted trouble and he would mark him with the red hot poker if it was off – off meaning if a row started with Jacky and Buster, though Jacky Reynolds was very small he was afraid of no one. I am pleased to say I spoke to Jacky without belittling him and eased the situation over, so the argument came to nothing.

If one went for a drink at the Spread Eagle pub on the corner of Shoreditch and went into the public bar one would probably see drinking at the bar Alfie Allpress, Sammy Lowe, Nobby Clark and Ernie Covely. Alf and Sam were over six feet tall and broad of shoulder, and in comparison Nobby and Ernie were only short in height. Nobby had served a couple of sentences for theft and violence and he was a friend of Frankie Frazer and Johnny Collins. Alf had had a lot of say in criminal circles and he was respected by all. At one time I was in Parkhurst Prison with Alf.

Sometimes I would go to the area of Soho to a club run by Peter Gillam and his brother and would possibly see Alf Gerrard at the bar. Alf came from Canning Town and was well known all over London. He had recently pulled a shooter on Buller Ward when they had been drinking in a club down the meat market. It was incidents like this that were spoken of as part of the underworld politics. This was not a liberty on the part of Alf as Buller Ward himself was also a capable villain. I would have a few gin and tonics with Alf and the Gillam brothers who had made me welcome and would then depart and perhaps go to the Pigalle Restaurant Club off Regent Street where I would order another gin and tonic. Scotch Jack Buggy would probably be sitting at a table close to the stage and Shirley Bassey would be singing from the stage and would captivate the audience. Buggy was a very flash villain and at one time he had been given a ten year sentence when he was convicted of shooting Big Charlie Reader outside the Pigalle Club. Buggy had shot Charlie Reader in the stomach and Charlie was lucky to live. Some years later Buggy went missing and has never been seen since.

Villains We Have Known

Jimmy Scott, The Aussie

Jimmy Scott was a friend of my old man's. He was an Australian con man whose alias was Jimmy Scott, The Aussie. Ever since our initial acquaintance, his facial appearance has never seemed to alter and he carried the aura of a forty-eight year old man. He had iron-grey hair and mischievous looking, twinkling blue eyes. With his lack of height and stout build, he could easily have been misconceived to be a businessman rather than a con. I first met him when he came to Vallance Road with my father after they had been out drinking. Jimmy Scott accepted the offer of a bed for the night instead of journeying back to Paddington where he lived. Many Aussies lived in the Paddington area at that time, it being a centre-point for Australian immigrants, and most survived by earning a living using their wits. The following morning when Jimmy Scott came down to breakfast, he gave Ron and I £50 each, which was a considerable sum in those days, especially to two teenagers, who never forgot this generous gesture. Jimmy acquired his money by resorting to confidence tricks which he had used all over the country. He would also ensnare the wealthy by involving them in high-stake card games on the railway trains; he would invariably win hands by playing dishonestly. His attire was always bulging with money. Jimmy was a heavy drinker, often frequenting our establishments, the Double R Club and The Kentucky where occasionally, although paralytic and staggering slightly, he still remained standing.

When I recall characters like Jimmy Scott, who enjoyed life so much, I find it hard to accept that they are no longer with us. His cue to life seemed to be his zest for living, which he achieved to the full before the door of death finally turned its key on him.

Tony Mulla and Alf Melvin

In the early days of 1960, I phoned a friend at a club in Gerrard Street and I was shocked when the friend told me of the deaths of Tony Mulla and Alf Melvin.

The story of these two people is one of the saddest I have ever known. 'Big' Alf Melvin was an ex-heavy-weight professional fighter and he was also a known villain. He was over six feet tall and was heavily built with powerful shoulders. He had thick grey hair, in fact more silver than grey, and he had a fighter's face. He was like a teacher to a pupil in his relationship with Tony Mulla.

Alf Melvin was about forty-five years of age. He was a gambling and drinking man and lived where he was born in Hackney, London.

Tony Mulla was about thirty-six years of age. He too was born and bred in Hackney, London. Like his teacher, Tony was also an ex-heavyweight fighter. He was over six feet tall and like Alf Melvin, Tony weighed over fifteen stone. He was a good-looking man with olive-coloured skin and had jet black, sleek hair and brown eyes. He was of Italian descent and a heavy gambling and drinking man.

Both Melvin and Mulla had gained fearsome reputations all over London because of their exploits as villains. Both had won many battles with other villains, but Tony Mulla had also been the sufferer at one time; he had been badly cut all over his body, when a firm of other villains had broken into his flat and attacked him.

Though Alf Melvin was the elder, it was Tony Mulla who was seen to be the one of high profile, and it was Tony who seemed to be in the position of a club owner, despite the fact that the different clubs and clip joints Tony and Alf controlled were of joint partnership. To those who were none the wiser, it seemed that Alf Melvin's position was being one of the doormen to these clubs and clip joints.

Alf had taught Tony everything he knew about gambling and various ways of earning money without working for anyone else, and they had been through years of adversity and happy times together. They could truly say that their friendship had matured like that of a very good wine over the years. They had both just taken control of various clip joints and pornographic shops in the Soho area of the West End of London and were at the height of joint success.

Alf Melvin was a man of great sensitivity and was known to brood on any occasion when he was slighted. Tony Mulla really loved life to the full and this was very apparent to me on the many times I had been in his company. I had also gone to the wedding of 'Big' Tony Mulla which was held in the area of Clerkenwell where most of those of Italian descent lived during this time. I recalled how I had seen and heard Alf Melvin, who was Tony's best man, give a very complimentary speech on the good qualities of his friend and pupil Tony Mulla, when I received the sad news that both were dead.

Sometime later I pieced together the story of what caused this great tragedy: It seemed that for some time, Tony Mulla had made derogatory remarks to Alf Melvin that made Alf feel inferior of position. I personally do not think that Tony meant any harm or realized what he was saying, but I found out that all this had been on Alf's mind for sometime.

On the morning in question, Tony Mulla and Alf Melvin had had some words and Alf Melvin pulled out a small revolver from his pocket and shot Tony Mulla two or three times. Tony managed to get down the stairs of the clip joint and lay in the gutter dying. It was said by passers-by that Tony uttered his last words and said, 'Save me because I don't want to die.' I believe this to be an accurate version of his last words because, as I previously stated, he did lead life to the full. After Alf Melvin had shot Tony Mulla, he put the gun to his temple, pulled the trigger and killed himself. It seems theirs was a classic example of the epitome of life's seesaw of sorrow and joy.

Billy Hill

When I was in my early twenties, the man I wanted to emulate most of all was the former gang boss of London's underworld, Billy Hill. The prime reason for my admiration was, that apart from Billy being very physical and violent when necessary, he had a good,

10

quick-thinking brain and this trait appealed to me most of all. Ron and I became very good friends with Billy Hill over the years and I learned a lot from him by observing his thoughts put into action.

One example concerns the time when Ron and myself, Charlie and a mutual friend Willie Malone were at Vallance Road. The phone rang and Ron took the call. It was Billy Hill who said to Ron, 'Will you come over to my flat as quickly as possible?' Ron replied, 'Okay Bill,' and replaced the receiver. Then Ron relayed the message: 'That was Billy Hill on the phone. I think he's got some kind of trouble. Let's get over there as quickly as possible.' Ron and I picked up a shooter each and the four of us departed. Charlie drove as we headed towards the vicinity of Bill's flat in Moscow Road, Bayswater. Upon our speedy arrival, Bill answered the door and invited us in. Ron said to Billy, 'What's the trouble, Bill? We've brought some shooters.' Bill laughed and gave us one of his smiles. We were assembled in his lounge and he said 'Hang on there a minute.' Then he left us for a moment and went to the bedroom. When he reappeared he tossed a wad containing £500 of brand new banknotes onto the table. 'Take that few quid for your trouble and cut it up between you. I was only testing you to see how fast you'd get over here, or if you'd blank the emergency.' This is just one instance of his great sense of humour and of his good thinking.

Another time, two fellas and myself went to the 21 Rooms in the West End and were refused admittance by the two doormen dressed in tuxedos. I struck one of them on the chin, and as he hit the deck, my two friends applied the same treatment to his partner who quickly joined him on the floor.

I immediately thought we may be arrested for

11

grievous bodily harm, due to the fact that one of the doormen may have recognized me. I also knew that Billy Hill procured a nice few quid out of the 21 Rooms for ensuring this type of situation didn't occur. Even though it was in the early hours, I decided that the best thing to do was to confront Bill, confess and explain the situation. He was home when we arrived and invited us in. I related my version of the affray and asked him if he could find out if charges were imminent. To my surprise, Bill was not the slightest bit perturbed that we had floored the doormen at the club, in fact his reaction was quite the opposite. He telephoned the owner of the 21 Rooms and said 'This is Bill on the phone, I hear you've just had some trouble at the club? I'm ringing to let you know I've taken care of it and you will not get any more trouble, just leave it to me. I'll pop in the club to see you tomorrow night.' He had been speaking to the club owner Harry Meadows, who along with his brother Bert, owned the place. The 21 Rooms was one of the most exclusive clubs in London at the time, and I believe the name 21 was assigned to it in reference to the 21 bedrooms it contained.

To get back to the story, having concluded this conversation, Bill replaced the receiver and seemed very pleased with himself. He handed me £300, again in crisp, new notes and said 'Take that few quid, it would have cost me more to have arranged such a commotion to ensure my services are still necessary,' and he smiled with a twinkle in his eyes. The point he was making was that he had turned disadvantage to advantage, and the next day he would probably receive five grand from the owners for preventing any further incidents happening. The probability of this seemed highly unlikely, as such an exclusive establishment didn't attract much trouble. Still, three tough guys from the East End had presented Bill with just the opportunity he needed to extort a few more quid out of the Meadows brothers. Again this was a classic example of how sharp Bill could weigh up a situation and turn it to his advantage. Billy Hill was respected all over London and one of his favourite haunts was an area called Warren Street where he used to associate with all the car dealers.

One time in his younger days he visited Johannesburg in South Africa, along with Bobby Ramsey, the ex-fighter. They were in a club one night and while Bill gambled, Ramsey watched. An argument started between Billy and the minder of the club, an ex-professional wrestler. The minder placed his hands on Bill's shoulders to throw him out, whereupon Bill drew a knife and cut him up so badly he needed one hundred stitches. Outside the club, Bill produced a revolver and aimlessly fired pot shots at one of the other guards. Ramsey was arrested for this offence and served three months in a South African jail, whilst Bill avoided capture and escaped back to London.

One time, Billy took a yacht to the port of Tangier. Two of his crew were Georgie Walker, the ex-light heavyweight fighter, now a successful businessman in London, and Eddie Chapman who during the War won the Iron Cross in recognition for his services as a British double agent. On arrival in Tangier, Bill and his motley crew were involved in a fight with some American sailors. Fists, bottles and chairs flew and as the Yanks lay sprawled about the bar where the fight had occurred; Bill and company were claiming a resounding victory.

To me, Billy Hill was the ultimate in what a

professional criminal should be like. He was not very muscularly built, but with a knife, he could be lethal. He was a smart dresser, a good host and the best of spenders. In his last days he became pretty much a recluse. Having travelled the world three times, he had seen and done almost everything. He died a millionaire at the age of seventy-three.

As a postscript to this story of my friend Billy Hill, I like to think, that in some ways I have come close to emulating him; to be honest, I acknowledge that he stands alone and there will never be another Billy Hill.

Old Villains

Ted Stannard

I will attempt to give an insight into all the villains we got to know over the years, so as to show what kind of people they were and how we looked upon some of them as local heroes.

I recall one particular day, when Ron and I had met with Jim Stannard in the Marquis of Cornwall public house at the top of Vallance Road, which joined Bethnal Green Road. It was during the afternoon drinking hours and Jim was expecting to meet his brother Ted in the public bar. Ted had just been released from Dartmoor Prison. He had been convicted of razor slashing the rent man who had called to collect the arrears owed. This incident, coupled with the consideration of his many previous convictions for violence – for he was a very impetuous character – resulted in him serving seven years. During this time at Dartmoor another con had smashed him in the jaw with an iron bar, consequently breaking it and dislodging several teeth. Ted would not consider prosecuting the con responsible, as it went against his own moral code; not to nick anyone, but to seek one's own revenge.

Ron, Jim and I did not have long to wait before Ted arrived. As he entered the door of the saloon bar, a silence fell across the room – his reputation still preceded him despite his seven-year exile and the locals still remained in awe of Ted. He looked very smart in his suit and waistcoat. Jim introduced him to us proudly, as though his brother had returned from a pilgrimage instead of doing seven years down the moor. Ron and I shook hands with Ted as we were genuinely pleased to meet him and had recognized his character since we were kids. But now, we were the ones upfront and Ted knew our reputation as well as we knew his. We gave Ted a few quid and the four of us enjoyed a few drinks together. Once when we met Billy Hill for the first time, he said 'Doesn't old Ted Stannard come from your manor, Bethnal Green?' and we said 'Yes' and Bill said 'If you ever see him give him my best wishes.' On this day, I recalled this and relayed Bill's message to Ted.

Johnny, The Greek

Ron and I were in Brixton Prison and one of the remand prisoners we became friendly with was a powerfully built young Greek fella. He was twenty-two years of age with dark curly hair and had once been a good, light heavyweight amateur boxer. Johnny was currently on remand for demanding money with menaces and by coincidence, we were on a similar charge. We exchanged addresses, his was in Camden Town, and agreed if we were acquitted, we would give him a job on the firm.

I'm glad to say we were exonerated and we found out that Johnny the Greek was vindicated on his charge too. I never did find out his surname, but in criminal circles in those days, surnames were unimportant. Most characters had aliases anyway, or were tagged with pseudonyms assigned to them for life, hence, Johnny the Greek. Upon his release, Johnny came to see us and as previously promised we employed him to stand on one of our club doors. This made him very happy as he was determined to go straight and keep within the law. One night I received the bad news that the twenty-three-year-old Greek had died from a heart attack, while running away from the police in the area of Soho after a club disturbance. The owner testified that Johnny had visited the club demanding money, but took to his heels when the police pursued him. I arranged his funeral and called at his parents' house in Camden Town to pay my last respects, where I was permitted to spend some time alone with him. He was laid out in an open coffin, looking so young with his wavy hair and his hands folded as if in prayer. I lent over the coffin and kissed him on the forehead and said the words 'Take it easy, you will be OK now.' You see, when I met him in Brixton, he told me he had a fear of being incarcerated in prison. I also discovered that although he had been chased by the police because of the club owner's allegations, the charges were not true. The owner was aware of John's past and was just being malicious towards him. Johnny the Greek was sadly missed by all of us.

Andy Paul

I was introduced to Andy Paul one night at Esmeralda's Barn. His reputation preceded him so I was aware of his character. He was around five feet ten inches tall, sturdily built with olive skin and dark wavy hair and of Italian descent. He had been working at a gambling club in Stoke Newington, but on this night he asked Ron and I if we could oblige him with employment as he wanted to be on the firm. His character was creditable, we knew he could look after himself, so we put him in charge of the Cellar Club below The Barn. We also gave him a job looking after Danny Green's speil in Kingsland Road of which we had half-shares. Andy would alternate between both clubs, driving his little white open-top sports car.

At twenty-three years of age, he was married with three children and resembled Johnny the Greek, in looks. He had real zest for life, speeding everywhere in his sports car as though he had a race against time and drinking, gambling and enjoying himself in general. He was particularly good at his job in the clubs and no one would try to take liberties while he was around.

One Monday he failed to show up at the Cellar Club and then to my sorrow I found out why. He had gone to his mother's house for the weekend to attend a wedding and an argument had developed between Andy and his brother Bonny. Though the details were rather nebulous, the fact remained that Andy had caught a shotgun blast in the stomach and collapsed with blood pouring from his wounds. He was rushed to the hospital and as they prepared him for surgery, a police sergeant tried to interview him. 'Tell us what happened son, we need to know so we can press charges.' But, true to his principles and code of life, Andy replied 'Fuck-off, it's nothing to do with you.' They were his last spoken words, he died seconds later.

An inquest was held and a verdict of accidental death was recorded. I attended Andy's funeral and as I stood at the graveside, the rain was pelting down on the beautiful flowers which adorned the coffin and I visualized Andy racing along the East End streets in his little white sports car. This nostalgic memory brought tears streaming from my eyes.

Dodger Mullins

Jack Mullins had been a villain all his life. Due to his endless evasion and side-stepping from the law's dragnet, he was credited with the moniker synonymous with his actions; Dodger Mullins. Not a particularly big man, Dodger stood around five feet six inches tall. He was slightly built with black curly hair, brown eyes, a broken nose and high cheekbones. His face also carried a couple of scars, the result of past knife fights he had been embroiled in.

Dodger lived in a block of flats adjacent to Vallance Road and was a friend of my old man's, consequently we became friends with him too. He was known all over London and Ron and I had the utmost respect for him for years. Since being a teenager, he used to be paid regular pensions of money from all bookmakers and publicans in the vicinity. His main criminal forte was that he was an excellent professional pickpocket. One time he received a seven-year sentence, for shooting out windows and at a rival villain by the name of Harding. He served his stint at Dartmoor, which at the time was considered to be the toughest jail in England. The fact that he had been committed to hard labour gave some indication of how difficult he was going to find it and subsequently he was involved, as one of the ringleaders, in the famous Dartmoor mutiny. For this misdemeanour, he received extra punishment which only contributed to making him a legend in the circles of London's underworld. Dodger's friend who helped him organize the mutiny was also renowned in the underworld. His name was Ruby Sparks from Finsbury Park, alias Rubberneck.

When Dodger was young, the governors of London were the Italian Sarbini brothers. Dodger and a firm he banded together, were travelling by coach to the Brighton Race Track for a showdown with the Sarbinis over who should control the racing pitches there, when their vehicle was stopped by the police. A routine search revealed that passengers were concealing shooters, knives and coshes about their persons. Dodger was sentenced to five years for his part in the incident.

One night I was in the Kentucky Club and at this date, Dodger was nearly seventy years of age. It was 1963 and he was in the club when Johnny Nash walked in with his mob, accompanied by Joey Pyle. John and Joe were old friends of ours, likewise the firm with him, but Dodger, unaware of the political situation at the time asked to speak to me privately. In the passageway of the club, I joined Dodger during the quiet interlude to hear what he had to say. 'If there's any trouble with that firm, I'll make one with you and Ron. I'm shootered up,' and he produced from his overcoat pocket a small black Italian Beretta. I said

'Thanks Jack, but it's not necessary, they are friends of ours. Come back into the bar and let me buy you a drink.' I told Ron about this gesture of loyalty on Dodger's part and I never forgot him for it.

He was a really game fella, even in his twilight years. His eventual demise was partly due to his good living and appetite for life. He had been out drinking with a friend, who was chauffeuring them around on a tour of local pubs, when the car was involved in an accident. Dodger was injured and taken to Bethnal Green Hospital where he lay for some weeks. Ron and I visited him, but very soon afterwards pneumonia set in and he died in the hospital.

Tiger Hardy

Tiger Hardy also resided in Bethnal Green and he too had been a lifelong villain. He was about five feet five, of average build and had still blue eyes and a broken nose. He had a habit of sniffing and would continuously wipe his nose with the back of his hand. It was more a reflex action than out of necessity. He also had a scar down the right-hand side of his face and walked with a perpetual limp due to the club-foot on his left leg.

Hardy was a man feared by many in the East End. Ron and I got to know him well although he was getting on in years when we made his acquaintance. He used to drive a pony and cart and wore a shirt in all weathers despite the temperature. Each lunchtime, he'd stop for a drink at The Crown and Anchor public house, leaving his horse and cart laden with rags outside. The horse would chew away contently at the oats in the nosebag and occasionally spray the cobblestone road with its urine. The steam would arise like an eruptive geyser, but the horse remained static and calm, continuing to masticate its food.

They called Tiger by that name because he had a ferocious temper just like his feline counterpart. He was another character we learned to admire, and seeing him riding the streets on his horse and cart each day, I likened his image to that of a cowboy.

Tommy Venables

Tommy Venables lived in Menotti Street, near Vallance Road. He was about five feet eight-and-a-half inches tall with blue eyes and had one of the worst razor slashes I have ever seen down the right-hand side of his face. He was a villain and a con man and had never done an honest day's work in his life. Tommy had a son, Shaun who was almost the same age as Ron and I and we became friendly with him as well as his father. At one time, Shaun, Ron and I were arrested for grievous bodily harm on the police, but this little story is about Tommy Venables, to show the type of people we were brought up with and who taught us the tricks of the trade.

Tommy Venables would select a likely client as a receiver of stolen goods and work on him what is known as 'The Comer' . He would offer to sell them a lorryfull of cigarettes and would arrange a meeting place to drop the load. His driver would deliver the goods and the receiver would climb up into the back of the lorry to inspect the merchandise. He would open one of the top cartons and take out, as a sample, a pack of cigarettes. Tommy would then get the buyer to hurry by intimating the possibility of the law's presence in the area. Invariably, the receiver would hastily get down from the vehicle and hand Tom the cash in exchange for the snout. Tommy would disappear as fast as possible from the area of transaction, as happy as a sandboy, knowing that he had made a successful con. The receiver would be unloading his consignment of stolen cigarettes speadily in anticipation of the police arriving. Tommy, by this time, would be in his local, downing a couple of large scotches in celebration and feeling a little more affluent. It was only when the dealer went to resell the cigarettes at a later date, did he discover to his amazement, that he had been duped and the cartons contained not tobacco, but sawdust!

The fact that Tommy was a well-known villain would most times ensure that the injured party did not go to the police, or seek any monetary reimbursement from him. Tommy Venables' reputation was too well-renowned to seek recompense. Another favourite ploy of a con trick that Venables used to do, as did many others in the East End including myself, was to go to the main dealer in snide rings, Red-faced Tommy. He would give us the rings on credit with one proviso attached – we looked after Redface himself when a sucker was found who would buy one of the imitation rings that looked genuine.

Tommy Venables sold many of these fake rings all over London, so in retrospect he was a lucky man only to bear the scar of one attack, especially when most of the capital's receivers had a heavy on their firm in anticipation of being targeted as suckers. I knew one East End face who used to sell the jargoons regularly.

Albert, The Jar

Albert, the Jar, so named because he sold so many jargoons, would laugh his way out of any situation if any receiver caught up with him after being taken for a ride. Once he had their money, the sucker had no chance of retrieving it. Albert was a real amiable fella and could charm his way out of any predicament others would regard as highly dangerous. His eyes would really sparkle when he made a score and touched for a few notes by taking someone on. I have often seen him drinking and cracking jokes with the people he had duped and you could guarantee before they parted, Albert would rectify the unpleasant atmosphere between them. He would say to them, 'There's my phone number, find me a customer for one of my jargoons and I will cut you in for a few quid.' The sucker would be so eager to get his money back, that he would go along with Albert's philosophy and feel quite blessed that he may be compensated. They would shake hands and part amicably.

One time when Albert was feeling under the weather and decided to visit his crooked doctor for some advice, I can assure you it wasn't his conscience playing him up. Albert used to say to me, 'When you find a mug, squeeze him like a lemon and leave him screaming. There's one walking over London Bridge every day.' Anyway, Albert saw his doctor and said

'For some reason or other, my nerve's shot up,' and the doctor replied, 'There's no wonder. I'm surprised you've never had a nervous breakdown. You go all over London, conning people left, right and centre, never knowing when any injured party may seek retribution and take a knife to you. You accept it as the norm to drink with these people, laughing and joking after you have relieved them of their money. It's a wonder you've never been found in a river or alleyway dead!' The doctor pointed out to his usually happy-go-lucky patient that his way of life was far from normal and eventually the stress of his dangerous living would catch up with him. Albert related this story to me one day while we were drinking at the bar in the Double R Club.

Always one for a great sense of humour, he seemed genuinely sorry for himself and said to me 'Those who work in factories for a living, don't know what peace of mind they've got!' Needless to say Albert, the Jar was one of my best customers at the Double R Club and if he should read this story, I hope he will contact me as I'm sure I can still find him a few punters.

Wassle Newman

The last time I saw Wassle Newman was on the corner of Cheshire Street some time in 1966. He was wearing a navy blue Crombie overcoat, looking extremely smart and he told me he had been to the funeral of one of his closest old friends.

Wassle was about five feet seven inches tall, very thickset with fair hair, still blue eyes and a slightly broken nose. He was a legend in the East End of London as a fighting man, and had the most beautiful set of white teeth, which he credited to eating hard crusts of bread. I once went to see Lionel Bart's show, 'Fings Aint What They Used To Be'. It was a show that revolved around East London characters and throughout the entire performance, Wassle's name was mentioned as the main character title of the show.

I've heard countless stories relating to Wassle, but the most humorous one concerns the night he went to the coffee stall which was parked at the Salmon and Ball in Bethnal Green. Wassle was a regular customer at the stall and the owner was conscious of his reputation. To preserve the harmony, he quite willingly gave Wassle a crust of bread each night with his cup of tea, to keep his teeth sharp and polished. One particular night, Wassle approached the stall for his usual order, to find the owner absent and a stranger in charge. Wassle requested his regular crust of bread and was politely told to 'Fuck-off!' by the manager who appeared to have no knowledge of him. Wassle was livid and flew into a cold rage while the vendor aimlessly went about his business. To enable the stall to be towed, it was connected to the van by a length of iron chain. Wassle disconnected the chain and attached it to a passing tram that was rolling along. As it dragged it behind, the stall and all its contents were smashed completely. Wassle was served up eighteen months for this little misdemeanour, but he had rectified a dent in his pride and promoted his notoriety by spreading it further afield.

Another time, he was in a caff and an argument

developed between him and a character he wasn't too fond of. Wassle said to the man, 'What's the time?' and the fella answered, 'Nearly twelve o'clock, midnight.' Wassle said 'Have you ever seen one day turn into the next?' and the man said 'No'. Wassle said 'You have now' and promptly hit the character across the head with a sauce bottle. When the injured man finally came to, it was the following day.

In the East End at this time, there was a lightweight fighter by the name of Alby Day, who used to be a title contender and boxed on Jack Solomon's bills. Alby Day was not unaccustomed to fighting in the street either. One lunchtime he and Wassle were in the local pub when an argument began. Wassle went to the toilet followed by Day and as he was relieving himself, Day slung a sly punch at Wassle that left him on the floor. Wassle recovered, left the public house and Day resumed drinking, falsely believing he had won the battle. A short time later, the saloon door opened and Wassle entered. Wrapped around his hands like a gauntlet was a long chain which he had taken from his horse and cart. He came up behind Day, unleashing the chain and with great ferocity coiled it around Day's neck. He dragged him outside and proceeded to haul him along the pavement. Once again, Wassle conserved his status and his reputation remained intact.

Another story reveals how he approached the owner of a fish shop for money but was refused payment. Wassle hastened away, but returned minutes later holding a cat by its throat. Without hesitation, Wassle threw the crying feline into the fry-pan, ensuring once again, that in future, regular payments would come his way from this particular establishment.

Jimmy Spinks

Jimmy Spinks was a close friend of my father. He epitomized everything a fighting man should be. Jimmy was around five feet nine with shoulders like an ox and a powerful neck to match. He had slightly fair hair, brown eyes and perfect teeth and his looks were complemented by his choice of clothing which was always impeccable. Jimmy's face had more scars from knife and razor slashes than any man I have ever seen, but this did not detract from his fighting ability. His distinction as a fighter was renowned, therefore any opponents he encountered always used implements to compensate for their inadequacy; without them they regarded the contest unbalanced.

Jimmy would often sit in the local pub in his shirt sleeves, with old-fashioned armbands wrapped around his huge biceps. One time he was a minder in a club in the West End, when a patron spotted him and offered to take him to Hollywood to star as a screen tough guy in motion pictures. Jimmy thanked the Hollywood producer but declined his invitation.

When we were kids, Ron and I would wait outside the Spread Eagle public house in Shoreditch for Jimmy to come out. He would take us next door to the sweet shop and buy us chocolate wrapped in silver foil, shaped like English currency, two shillings and six-pence pieces. None of these fighting men, Jimmy Spinks, Wassle Newman or the others, were liberty-takers and all respected and were kind to women and children. One of my personal regrets, to a lesser degree, is that I did not spend more time in the company of all these fighting men.

Tommy Brown

Tommy Brown came from Tottenham and was known as 'The Bear'. He was around five feet eleven and carried the most powerful shoulders I've ever seen on a man. His neck was nineteen inches thick and he had steel-grey hair, blue eyes and a pugilist's nose. He was known as 'The Bear' because of his size and was regarded as a fighting man in and out of the ring. Tommy was also a member of the Kray firm. I valued him as my closest friend out there in the sixties and we were inseparable. At every opportunity we would go into the backyard at Vallance Road and spar with the gloves on. Tommy had been a good professional heavyweight fighter and he usually assisted me on the doors of our clubs to keep order. His presence was a deterrent to would-be trouble-makers who didn't fancy their chances against Tom in a brawl. I once prevented him from breaking the jaw of Billy Daniels, the coloured singer, when he became impertinent towards Tom. At the Double R Club one day, a customer became rather raucous and disruptive. Tommy lifted him by his tie and swung the fella round the club like an awny yo-yo.

Just as Jimmy Spinks and Wassle Newman were smart dressers, so was big Tommy Brown. He dressed like a film star and played the part well. All the firm held him in high esteem and always referred to him as 'Big Tom' or 'The Bear'. The police once called at Tom's Tottenham address to arrest him. Before they succeeded in taking him in, The Bear knocked out eleven officers. For this he received a sentence of two years.

As I write this I am sadly doubtful if I will ever see

him again, but my thoughts are with Big Tom as I write and muse about the past.

Ted Machent

Ted Machent, alias 'Long Legs', came from Upton Park. He was a handsome fella with dark curly hair and a very athletic, sprightly way of walking. He was a regular villain never having done a day's work in his life and for a time he was a member of Jack Spot's firm. Machent had the awesome reputation of being someone who could turn very violent in a row.

When the big bullion robbery of the 1950s took place at London Airport, he was the only participant to successfully evade capture. He was present at the scene of the crime when the waiting police swooped, but Ted had the presence of mind to cling to the axle beneath the Black Maria. Tenaciously he held his position as the van departed the area, desperately waiting for the driver to decelerate before he could release his grip and roll to eventual freedom. His intrepid performance resulted in him receiving burn marks on his palms and fingers, but he carried these wounds like a medal, a constant reminder of his own private war. The rest of his friends were not so lucky. George and Jimmy Woods, Sammy Josephs and others were in a fierce police battle and received twelve and ten-year sentences for their involvement. Such verdicts were unheard of in those days, but the gold bullion was estimated to be worth one million pounds, a king's ransom in the fifties.

Ted was a friend of mine, and a regular patron at the Double R Club where he got up to all kinds of tricks whilst drinking. I have witnessed him holding three large light ale glasses in one hand and filling them to the brim from a bottle in the other, without incident. He would also clear the bar with one stride which was a bit of a feat.

Ted was also known as 'The Cavalier' due to his style of living. I am sad to say that it was this lifestyle that ironically terminated his existence at forty-five years of age. I read about his death while I was at Parkhurst. Apparently, he was involved with a woman and during an argument with her son, a shotgun was produced and the offspring blasted Ted in the stomach. The Cavalier laughed no more.

Georgie and Jimmy Woods

Georgie and Jimmy Woods also hailed from Upton Park. Jimmy is no longer with us but George still remains one of my closest friends. Both brothers were about five feet-and-a-half inches tall and thickset. George has a scar down the right-hand side of his face where an assailant had used an open razor on him. Jimmy and George were villains and two of the best thieves in the country but unfortunately they spent years at Dartmoor Prison. Jimmy and George were committed to twelve and ten years respectively for their part in the bullion robbery.

When George was slashed with an open razor he remained true to his code of living by refusing to prosecute his attacker, preferring to bide his time and punish the culprit himself. One dark night, George huddled in a doorway down a remote alley, waiting for the offender to pass. As the man drew alongside the opening, George leapt out and struck him repeatedly with an iron bar. The infliction was so severe that the victim required a steel plate attachment in his skull for the rest of his life.

These types of vendettas were commonplace in the London scene of yesteryear. Within criminal circles a code of silence was always maintained and legal action was never considered. The victim would either blank the incident or wait for an opportunity to punish the transgressor himself. These were the regulations of the concrete jungle; the rules of the big city; the law they all abided by.

George and Jimmy were two of the best spenders in London and were admired and respected by everyone. Today George runs his own fruit stall in East London, preferring to leave all his criminal activities behind him.

Jack and Ray Rosa

Jack and Ray Rosa both came from the Paddington area. These two brothers were friends of Ron and I, often patronizing our club, The Double R. They were also friends of the late Billy Hill. Jack had served time in prison and at one stage was a Broadmoor patient, but both brothers were immensely likeable fellas. Ray is also known to be one of the best punters in the

London gambling circuit. Both men were known to be staunch, determined types. Undaunted by intimidation, no one took liberties with them as they'd back off from nobody. In criminal terms, this translates as they would 'swallow with no one'.

When Jack was involved in a car crash on the M1, the car was written off. The accident occurred on a desolate stretch of highway. Jack, racked with the pain of having practically every bone in his body broken, crawled half a mile desperately seeking assistance. The doctors said it was a superhuman effort on the part of Jack Rosa and were astonished that he had the indomitable strength and fortitude to cover the half mile he'd crawled. Unfortunately Jack's injuries were too severe and he passed away. Billy Hill, Ron and I attended Jack's funeral along with his brother Ray.

At one time Ray was proprietor of a drinking club in the area of Balham High Street and my late wife Frances and I would visit the club to take a drink with Ray. He was a perfect gentleman to us, and that's how I shall always remember him. We have not been in touch for many years, but even now I consider Ray a good friend.

Bobby Warren

Bobby Warren was convicted and sentenced to seven years' imprisonment in the 1950s. He had been found guilty of slashing the face of Jack Spot, one of the former bosses of London during that era. This incident was a result of gangland warfare. Bobby Warren served the majority of his sentence at Wormwood Scrubs. Ron and I always got on well with him and he was a good friend to Billy Hill. I heard about his reputation when I was in my early twenties. Bobby was around ten years older than Ron and I and a well-known face in the London circles along with his constant companion Albert Dimes, alias Italian Albert, another London boss. Soho was the particular area where Dimes and Warren could be located. On my last holiday before this one, I vacationed in Tangier with Ron. Bobby Warren, his wife and family were over there, too, visiting Billy Hill and his wife, Gypsy. Bobby was always a quiet man and didn't take liberties either.

I write of all these people who were relevant to the London scene during the fifties and sixties and when I mention them, it must be remembered that I am only scratching the surface of my memory where these individuals are concerned. I could write volumes pertaining to their indiscretions and criminal activities, but I wish to protect the privacy of those still alive. Even if I did consider to write more about the deceased, it would take many volumes to recount the memories. A great many of my secrets will die with me solely to protect any serving party from the police and prosecution.

Albert Dimes

Albert Dimes was the central figure in the Soho area. He owned a betting shop there and Henry Cooper the former heavyweight champion of Britain, was often seen in the company of Italian Albert. Albert was a regular fight-fan and was present at all the main tournaments. He towered over six feet tall with sleek black hair and elegant and handsome features generated by his Italian lineage. Albert controlled the racing pitches at the point-to-point meetings all over the country. He always ensured that Ron and I had decent pitches at the courses. Albert was a very likeable person with a pleasing personality and a tendency to chain-smoke incessantly. Ron and I were in his betting shop and the gloves that Mohammed Ali and Henry Cooper fought with were hanging on the wall. Albert took them down from their place of distinction and presented them to me as a gift.

One of the last meetings with Italian Albert took place in Soho when he and I had a rendezvous with the Mafia boss from Philadelphia, Angelo Bruno. Since then, both men have given up the ghost. Bruno was blasted to death as he sat in a car in Philadelphia and Italian Albert Dimes died of cancer.

Bar

Ron and I used to visit the Vienna Rooms when we were in our early twenties. The rooms were directly behind Edgware Road and opposite the police station. They were situated on the second floor of the building. Jack Spot and his firm were the first to invite us there, it being one of the central establishments where all the key con men, gamblers and club owners would assemble.

One club owner who constantly visited was a tall slim coloured fella with gleaming white teeth by the name of 'Bar'. His left ear was minus a chunk, the result of a fight when an adversary had bitten it off. Bar was an effervescent character, full of pep and a representative of the old school. When we first made social contact with him, he had just completed a seven year term for shooting someone. Bar was well respected in the West End of London and in those days, it was a rare sight to see a coloured person circulating in such company. At one stage he owned the greyhound dog, Bar's Choice, which won the Greyhound Derby.

It was from this school of people that Ron and I imbibed all our knowledge and formed our style from an amalgamation of characters. In that era, they truly were riveting personalities to be associated with.

Johnny Nash

Johnny Nash is one of our best friends and the same age as Ron and I. He originates from the Angel Islington and we have known him since we were sixteen years old. We met in Shepton Mallet Prison where all three of us were serving a term of Army imprisonment. John was and still is, one of the best fighting men in the London area. He had the physique of an athlete and the looks and high cheekbones synonymous with the actor Jack Palance.

Johnny, one of seven brothers, is credited with having played a dominant role in the politics of the changing scene over the years in the capital. I was in Wandsworth Prison with him when he was serving two years for possessing a gun. He told me he had been fitted up on this charge and I have every reason to believe him.

Johnny is a compulsive gambler and I recall one evening, when he was playing in a West End casino and an ex-wrestler tried to take a liberty with him. Johnny picked up a chair and smashed it over the perpetrator's head until he had little inclination to wrestle anyone again. Johnny and his family used to look after the Bagatelle Club in the West End, another favourite haunt amongst many.

Harry Mellaship

Harry Mellaship was a friend of my father's and was roughly the same age as him but Ron and I considered him to be our friend, too. He came from Hackney and was recognized as a fighting man. Just under six feet tall, he was truly handsome and walked with the grace and agility of a tiger. Like many of the previous characters mentioned, Harry was a beau when it came to attire, and his mode of raiment would benefit any Hollywood actor. Harry Mellaship was a man of routine and around seven o'clock each morning he would take his customary stroll down Leabridge Road. He had never been cut by a weapon in any of his fights but when approaching his sixtieth year, a Scotsman by the name of Billy Quinn slashed him very badly down the side of his face. This unjustifiable attack provoked a lot of anger from the police in the London area. Quinn eventually received his comeuppance when Bobby Mutt, the son of one of Harry's friends, confronted him in a North London pub and the balance was redressed. Mellaship refused to press charges, denying any knowledge of his attacker. Nevertheless, Quinn was sentenced to three years for the laceration on Harry's face.

People like Harry Mellaship, his friend Bobby Mutt and Bobby Mutt Junior had a charisma that is hard to define to the reader. Suffice to say, they were larger-than-life characters and I felt priviledged to be accepted into their company and to fully appreciate their qualities. The ambience of being in these people's company was reminiscent of a Hollywood saga, a glimpse of which I am trying to instil into the readers' minds via my memory recall. I hope my portrayal of these individuals serves as credit to their memory and to reiterate that any vendettas between them were contained in their own criminal fraternity, involving no innocent party.

John Hall

Ron had just been sentenced to three years in prison with his two co-defendants, Billy Jones and Bobby Ramsey, who received three and seven years respectively. I was acquitted. The trial took place at the Old Bailey in 1957 and the verdict was imposed due to the

Right: Taken at the RR Club left to right Big Tommy Brown, Reg Kray & George Osbourne

Below: Violet Kray, Barbara Windsor & George Mullins

Below: Billy Hill (left) & George Walker (right)

Reg Kray, Joe Louis & Ronnie Kray

Above RR Club in Gymnasium – centre: Ted Kid Lewis, Billy Hill,
Terry Spinks & Terry Allen

Arthur Mason, Reg Kray Tommy Brown & Bobby Ramsey

Sulky Gowers, Red Faced Tommy, Jacky Reynolds, Ted Machent & George Woods

George Woods

Billy Hill

Below: Alberto Dimes alias Albert Dimes Italian Albert

Left: Reg Kray & George Woods

Left: One-armed Lou with Ron & young Barry Thompson

Below: Geoff Allen, Noelle Kurylo, Annie Allen & Frank Kurylo

Above: Reg, Squibbie & Ronnie

Above: Willie Malone & Charlie Kray

Right: Geoff Allen, Johnny Cardew, Ron Kray & club owner

Reg & Ron Kray

Selwyn Cooney pictured behind the bar in his club. Selwyn was from Leeds and was shot in the Pen Club murder.

Jack Spot

Soho Rangers FC: left to right: includes Stanley Baker, George Wisbey, William Stayton, Tommy McCarthy (Bert's brother), Albert Dimes, Frankie Frazer. Front row: Bert McCarthy, boxing promoter, Eddie Richardson and others

Geoff Allen & daughter

Freddie Foreman

Charlie Kray, Reg Kray & Freddie Foreman

Reg & brother Charlie

Charlie & Eddie Richardson

George Osbourne & Reg

Jack Spot

Ronnie & Mr Bill

left to right: Joe Pyle,
Reg Kray, Joe Louis,
Alex Stein, Ron Kray &
Tommy Cowley

Noelle Kurylo, Danny La Rue &
Frank Kurylo

Frank Kurylo &
Eric Mason

Bobby Ramsey

fourth from left: Teddy Smith with his hand on the singer Danny Williams, fourth from right: Jimmy Clark, Reg Kray & far back is Limehouse Willy

Ronnie Knight, Barbara Windsor & Reg Kray at the premiere of *Sparrows Can't Sing*

Reg wearing a scorpio tie pin

left to right: Albert Nichols Junior, Big Pat Connelly, fourth from left: Billy Thomas, Barney Ross, Billy Exley, Joe Schaffer & Albert Donoghue

stabbing with bayonets of Terry Martin. Terry and Jackie Martin were brothers from Watney Street, who belonged to a dockers gang which challenged our authority. During the inevitable fracas, Terry Martin was stabbed and unhesitatingly prosecuted us all.

I was in the Double R Club one afternoon, shortly after purchasing it, when a band of men came in and I bought them a drink. One was a fella by the name of John Hall, a fair-haired, robust type of chap, a familiar acquaintance and likeable rogue. John beckoned me over, and during our conversation, quite nonchalantly said, 'If you like Reg, I'll shoot them slags the Martins for nicking your brother and the other two.' I said to him 'Thanks John, I appreciate the offer, but I'll take care of it my own way. At this present time, it doesn't suit me for either of them to be shot, nevertheless I won't forget your gesture.' We continued drinking and after that day John became a regular visitor to the club.

Approximately six months later I picked up a national newspaper and the headlines read, 'East End gunman shot dead.' As I continued to read, the paper gave a fragmented account of John's demise, the rest I pieced together via the local grapevine.

John Hall had been arrested on several occasions and placed in the cells which triggered off his claustrophobia condition. These attacks became more severe each time he was incarcerated and consequently his hatred towards the law increased. On the day prior to his death, the police had called at his address in Ilford, East London, to take him to the station for questioning, but on this particular day they were unlucky and returned without their man. John, over a period of time had accumulated an arsenal of weapons. He was an avid collector, and had gun types of every description. On the evening following the police visit he moped about the house, brooding about the old bill and envisaging the spartan dungeon he loathed so much. In the confusion of his mind, his fate seemed sealed, all he had were a few precious hours to deliberate what course of action he would take. The following afternoon around two o'clock, John walked to the police station and entered. The only officer present was the desk sergeant. John reached into his pocket, pulled out a revolver and shot him dead before turning round and walking straight out. He ran down the road until he reached a phone booth were he paused to make a call. A short time later, resounding shots were heard and John Hall lay dead with a bullet in his brain. The police reported suicide, but local opinion differed, disputing the allegation and suggesting the police themselves were responsible for John's death. I can't comment on this as I was not a witness to the shooting; I am relating the story as it was told to me.

In retrospect, I often wonder what kind of job he would have done had I accepted his offer to shoot the Martins. There is one thing of which I am certain and that is, when it came to handling a gun, John Hall was very capable.

One-Armed Lou

Everyone in London's criminal and gambling fraternity identified Lou by this name. He came from Hackney and stood around five feet nine inches tall with dark wavy hair and classic features. His clothes complemented his persona, he dressed formally and resembled a film star. Lou lost his arm when he was just a child, yet fought against adversity and discrimination to achieve the objectives which so many of us take for granted. He learnt to drive a car, play snooker, swim to the extent of diving from the top board, and he even became a proficient tic tac at the races.

On one occasion at the billiard hall in Mare Street, a fella tried to take a liberty with him over a game of snooker. Lou retaliated by hitting the man over the head with a cue and killing him. He was arrested and was served an eighteen-month jail sentence.

Jimmy Essex

One day during my exercise period at Wandsworth Prison, I happened to catch sight of Ray Rosa speaking to Jimmy Essex. Little Jim, as he was known, came from West London. He was five feet tall, but his lack of height was more than compensated by his large heart, especially when it came to physical contact. While in prison, two strapping muscular cons had tried to take liberties with the diminutive lion and he'd stabbed them to death. Both murders occurred on separate occasions and on each charge, Jim was found guilty of manslaughter and given six and seven-year sentences to run concurrently with the one he was already serving. He already had a conviction for killing someone while in the throes of a robbery. Jim's looks

41

were deceptive. He could be as genial as the next person when left alone but when intimidated or provoked, his impulsive streak controlled his actions. One night in the Regency Club a Scotsman offended him so he picked up a drinking glass and smashed it into the man's face, completely dislodging his eye from its socket.

When I was walking round the exercise yard with him in Wandsworth, I invited him to my homecoming party when I was released. True to his word, Jim showed up at the celebrations held at the Queen's Hall in Commercial Road. The evening's entertainment was provided by the Clark Brothers who performed a dance routine. A host of celebrities mingled with the guests, eminent personalities like Len Harvey, the former professional light heavyweight champion of the world, the legendary boxer Ted Kid Lewis, Terry Spinks the former featherweight champion and Tom Driberg, the late MP, were a few amongst others, too numerous to mention.

Billy Bligh

The late Cassandra, the *Daily Mirror* columnist, once wrote an article on the funeral of Billy Bligh. Billy, a total villain, hailed from Clerkenwell in North London. He was good friends with Italian Albert, Bobby Warren and Frankie Frazer. Ron and I spent time with him on remand in Brixton Prison and saw him regularly at race tracks all over the country. He was a smaller man than Jimmy Essex, with a bald head, high cheekbones and hollowed cheeks caused by the ulcers from which he suffered. His eyes were inertly blue and through their intensity, one could perceive he was a man who did not tolerate fools. With his gaunt, frail appearance, one could easily misjudge his personality, for concealed beneath the superficial exterior was one of the most ruthless villains ever to be born in London.

Many feared Billy Bligh with good reason. He was a cold, calculating, vicious rogue. During our time with him in Brixton Prison, I observed him each day performing press-ups on the floor of his cell. He had numerous convictions for slashing the faces of policemen. His favourite implement was the open razor, and when Jack Spot was attacked by a rival gang outside Hyde Park Mansions, Billy Bligh was one of the ring leaders responsible for causing the most damage to Jack's face, slashing it to ribbons. His reward for this unmerciful attack was four years in prison, his last jail sentence. Billy Bligh died in prison due to his ulcer which never received the correct treatment it needed. At his funeral, which Cassandra reported on, villains from all over London congregated, taking with them many wreaths and flower displays.

It must be remembered that when I write about the violence of yesteryear, it is not because I revel in or condone this type of behaviour. In all honesty, I deplore unnecessary terrorism, especially when it is inflicted on innocent victims. When giving an insight into these characters' lifestyles, I try to do so in a dispassionate and objective way which is necessary if I am to portray the true ambience of the era and criminal fraternity. If the rapists and child molesters of today had committed their heinous attacks then, the Billy Blighs would have cut and mutilated their bodies beyond recognition. The reader may consider that to be rough justice, but I'm certain that if vigilantes of Bligh's calibre were present in today's society, these offences would be reduced dramatically. The transgressors would be more deterred by this form of retribution than by the lenient sentences they receive from the courts.

Frankie Frazer

Frankie Frazer is now a retired con after having spent over twenty years in prison. He acquired the alias Mad Frank due to his time spent as a patient at Broadmoor. Since his teenage days, he has always been a force to be reckoned with in the criminal underworld, and until his retirement he remained one of the top men in the London scene. He received a fifteen-year jail sentence for his part in the famous Richardson trials and a few years earlier served seven years for his involvement in the Jack Spot attack. Prior to his arrest in the Richardson case, he was present at the shoot-out at Smith's Club in Catford and suffered a bullet wound in the leg, which left him temporarily crippled. Frankie was also incriminated in the well-known Parkhurst Prison riots.

I must mention the loyalty of Frank's sister, Eva, towards her brother. It is common knowledge to anyone who knows them, how she stuck by her brother over the years. Five feet seven with sleek black hair, Frankie Frazer was regularly seen at all the best nightspots in the fifties and sixties.

Jack Spot

John Spot, the former Jewish boss of London, was born in Aldgate, East London in the early 1930s and christened Jack Comer. Today he must be around seventy-six years of age. In his younger days, he was a powerful figure of a man, with looks and features synonymous with Al Capone. He was very clean living and abstained from taking alcohol or cigarettes, although sometimes he'd take the occasional cigar. Though he was very affluent, one of Jack's bad points was that he tended to be rather parsimonious and not a liberal spender. Still, his fascinating personality cancelled out his frugality.

Initially, Ron and I got to know him well in our early twenties when he gave us pitches at the races. In the early 1950s when I was around twenty-one, I travelled up to Manchester with Jack, accompanied by George and Jimmy Woods. Spot had arranged a rendezvous at the Grand Hotel with the boss of a pac-a-mac company and came away from the meeting four grand richer. On the return journey to London by train, he handed me £25. As a novice to the business, I accepted the paltry sum with indignation, but held my tongue – I was learning. Many years later Jack opened a club in the West End of London and I arranged for someone to set fire to it. Despite this course of action, I still retain a fond memory of Jack's significant role during those years.

In the fifties, when he and Albert Dimes had a knife fight in a greengrocer's in central Soho, the account hit the headlines. Spot received very bad lacerations down the right-hand side of his face and suffered stab wounds also. Both men were arrested for causing an

45

affray and sent to trial. Two famous hearings resulted from this case, but each time the jury found both men innocent and they were acquitted. The entire episode was consequently known as 'the fight that never was'.

Billy Howard

Billy Howard in his early fifties was considered to be the governor of South London. He was a left-handed fighting man with the south paw stance and was regarded as one of the best street fighters in London. With a knife in his hand Billy was particularly vicious. He was around five feet eight-and-a-half inches tall, of medium build, and often wore a blue serge suit and white tie. His manners were impeccable and he spoke very eloquently. He was friendly with Wilfred Bramble and Harry H. Corbett, alias 'Steptoe and Son', the actors and Harry would often give Billy money. Billy looked after Winstons Club in the West End of London, but at one time he had a gambling club in Brixton Market. He was a genial host and whenever I visited he made me very welcome. Billy was a regular racegoer too, and we would often meet each other socially at the tracks.

Charlie and Eddie Richardson

Charlie Richardson and his brother Eddie, both from South London, became infamous for what was called 'The Richardson Torture Gang'. Charlie was sentenced to twenty-five years for the alleged crimes and Eddie received ten for grievous bodily harm.

Ron and I first encountered Charlie Richardson in the Army prison at Shepton Mallet where we were all serving sentences. I later served time with Eddie Richardson at Leicester Prison in 1971. We were both in the security block and passed the time by playing table tennis together, while the tabloid newspapers still reported the feuding rivalry between the Kray and Richardson gangs. I met up with Charlie again at Parkhurst years later and his sense of humour, which always appealed to me, had not been lost. When he finished work for the day in the prison workshop, he sought the comfort of his favourite armchair, refusing to move for anyone or anything. He even designated someone to make him pots of tea throughout his reclination and was content to sit there until it was time for him to be locked up in the seclusion of his own cell. Both brothers keep in touch with Ron and I and I hope that sometime in the near furture, we will all join together on the outside for a drink or two.

Freddie Foreman

I was first introduced to Freddie Foreman at a boxing

tournament. Aside from being of a similar age, we both shared a love of boxing and Freddie was a professional middleweight fighter. He also had a drinking club in the Old Kent Road, which I frequently patronized, as I enjoyed his convivial company. Freddie was very unfortunate to receive a ten-year sentence during the Kray trials of the sixties. He was found guilty of being an accessory after the fact to murder, along with my brother Charlie, who also received ten years. They were both convicted on the evidence of Ronald Hart, a habitual liar. Freddie was in Leicester Prison at the same time as Eddie Richardson and I, and we trained together in the gym. Before we parted company, we had both gained certificates for weightlifting.

Fred Foreman is a very honourable person. One time during the 1960s, Jimmy Murray, alias 'Irish Jimmy' had a clip joint in the West End of London. Five tearaways went to this clip joint and smashed up the chairs and tables and demanded money from Jimmy. Jimmy was a friend of Fred Foreman, and phoned him to tell him about the tearaways. Fred decided to help Jimmy and he, my brothers Charlie, Ron and I, went with Fred to the clip joint, sat down at the tables and had a drink. We had not been in the place long when the five tearaways entered and started to demand money. Fred, Charlie, Ron and I waited for them to hurl a chair through the air and then we went into action. We knocked out all five of them and scuffled them by the coat collars and dumped them outside the front of the clip joint. Jimmy Murray never had any more problems with anyone again.

Eric, The Horse

Eric, The Horse came from Walthamstow but was of German origin. He would terrorize the stallholders in Walthamstow market for protection money and on one occasion when one refused to meet his demands, he hacked three of his fingers off with a chopper. Eric, The Horse was a very fortunate man to escape the wrath of Ron and his retinue who went to seek him in the market. One day Ron and his friend Willy Malone banded a firm of around twenty men together and scoured the area for Eric, to ask him to exterminate the extortion racket he was running. Eric was a very lucky man for them to have missed him that day.

It's funny how times change, but if I met him today, I'd buy him a drink. They say we mellow with age, which is true, but it seems that people we connect with our youth, we miss as we grow older, probably because they are such a significant part of our past and apparent change was hardly imminent then. We tended to lose ourselves in complacency and flowed along with the tide of time, carrying on, never realizing until we looked behind, that we have all drifted further than we anticipated and our lives are drowning in dreams and memories. Hence, my succinct rendition of Eric, The Horse was only in passing as I sit here and muse about the past.

George Dixon

George Dixon from West Ham was six feet tall with
blond hair. His physique was complemented by his
broad shoulders which supported his height. He was
an accomplished fighter and had knocked many rivals
out with a single punch. At one time Dixon was in The
Rising Sun public house in Roman Road, when a fella
accosted him with a sawn-off shotgun in full view of
everyone. George calmly pushed the weapon aside,
floored the fella with one punch and claimed the gun.
Big George, as he was fondly called, has been hit on
the head, had his face slashed, been shot at and served
time in prison yet he still survived. Not long after we
were sentenced, George and his brother Alan were
both jailed for twelve and ten years respectively, for
allegedly demanding money in the London area.

The luckiest result Big George ever had, was when
fate played a hand that I should be there to save his
life. Ron had warned George to stay out of the
Regency gambling club, but in the morning George
disobeyed Ron's advice and entered with two friends. I
watched Ron's reaction; his face went white with
anger. He eased himself from the chair on which he
was sitting and headed for the men's room where I
knew he kept a revolver hidden in the top of the
cistern. Presently, he re-entered the casino area and
stared at Dixon. He nonchalantly pulled the gun out of
his pocket and calmly raised it in the air, lining it up
with the intention of shooting Dixon in the head. I
acted on impulse and grabbed the gun handle, causing
it to fall towards the floor. As it came to rest, I heard a
click and shouted out a warning to Dixon, 'Fuck-off!'
Dixon grasped the immediate danger he was in and he

and his companions took to their heels like rabid dogs being pursued by a hosepipe. Ron and I then had an argument as to why I interfered in his personal business. When Ron opened the gun we saw the firing pin had put an indentation in the bullet, but for some reason it hadn't gone off. Sometime later when Ron and George had patched up their differences, Ron presented George with the bullet to keep as a souvenir.

My Grandfathers, Jimmy Lee and Jimmy Kray

Both my grandfathers were fighting men. My paternal grandfather, Jimmy Kray, was born in Hoxton, Shoreditch. He was five feet nine and had strapping muscular shoulders on him. He was sometimes known as Mad Jimmy Kray. During the First World War, Jimmy had been machine-gunned in the legs but his fortitude ensured a speedy recovery with no lasting effects. He once told me he slept with an iron bar beneath his pillow to cosh anyone who crept up on him while he was sleeping. His reputation as a fighting man was generated because of his many street battles.

Jimmy Lee, my maternal grandfather was very much a man of the same fighting calibre. He was around five feet seven with a wiry frame but he could pack a punch using either hand, with equal velocity. Jimmy had been a bare-knuckle fighter on the docks and also fought professionally for a living. He was also an entertaining song-and-dance man and would walk on the tops of bottles, even though they stood at a precarious height. I have often seen him lick a white hot poker without burning his tongue. Had the poker been red and not white, with the tremendous amount of heat it contained, he most certainly would have been tongue-tied! I wouldn't advise anyone to try it. One time during an air raid in the War, Jimmy erected a stage in the shelter and presented a show. As he was performing his own inimitable style of dancing, he misjudged the stage distance and fell off the side of the platform with an almighty crash! Jimmy's repertoire certainly brought the house down, in more ways than one. The audience screamed with laughter as they momentarily disregarded the belligerent enemy outside.

The residents of the East End were united in this spartan sanctuary and the community spirit manifested itself as they graciously acknowledged the gregarious Jimmy Lee.

Geoff Allen

Ron and I first became friends with Geoff Allen over thirty-five years ago. It is a strange but interesting story how our paths crossed, and I will attempt to recount the events which led to our friendship and brought Geoff into our family as a considered uncle.

One particular night Ron and I were sitting in the Vienna Rooms, drinking coffee and enjoying the social banter, when Moiser Blueboy, a recognized villain on Jack Spot's firm, approached and put a proposition to us. 'Do you fancy a ride in the country? I found a mug farmer that I am going to take a few quid off in a crooked game of cards. He lives in Bishop's Stortford, near Stansted Airport, so if you fancy coming for a ride, I'll give you both a few quid when I relieve the mug of his money.' Blueboy incidentally, was one of the best shady card players in the country, so in anticipation of our palms being greased with his ill-gotten lucre at the break of day, we accepted his invitation. Also accompanying us were Sammy Leda-man and Johnny Stracey, another West End charac-ter. John drove the car following Geoff Allen, the nominated mug farmer, as he led the way in his own vehicle. We drew to a halt outside a quaint little cottage near Bishop's Stortford. The address was 11, Smith's Green, Geoff Allen's residence. Geoff invited us into his cosy little habitat and the game commenced without further ado. Geoff and Blueboy opted to play gin rummy while we sat and spectated. Ron and I were twenty years of age and we watched closely as the inscrutable Blueboy flawlessly dealt the cards.

All this was experience and every action and reaction I tried to digest for future reference. When Geoff Allen left the room, Blueboy would wink at us and certify that he still had control over the game and would 'take the sucker for a nice few quid'. The game continued until the early hours when they called it a day. Blueboy, true to his word, had come up trumps and fiddled Geoff Allen to the tune of £1100, a substantial amount in those days. Geoff seemed to accept defeat graciously but said to Moiser that he would be unable to pay his debt until the bank opened at ten o'clock. As he had work to do, he suggested we wait for him at the White Hart Inn in the centre of the village and he'd meet us there at eleven o'clock.

Blueboy and the rest of us were jubilant at the thought of our good fortune, and on reaching the hotel ordered a celebration breakfast each, to toast our success.

The adage 'time flies' is in fact a reality, but that morning as we anxiously awaited the arrival of Geoff Allen, time stood still, especially when the proposed hour of meeting came and went and the man didn't show. None of us seemed unduly suspicious over Geoff Allen's delay. Blueboy's assurance that he was just a gullible farmer had been justified, he suspected no undercurrent or subterfuge at all. Moiser decided to give Geoff a call and find out the reason for his delay. Geoff Allen answered the phone and told Blueboy that in no uncertain terms that he had no intention of paying him and if he made any attempt to go near the cottage, he was waiting with a shotgun and wouldn't hesitate to use it. As we watched Blueboy on the phone it was obvious something was wrong by the expression on his face. He replaced the receiver as though it were a lifeline and he was suffering from a cardiac arrest. As he related the conversation he'd had with Geoff Allen to us, our ebullience subsided like a deflated balloon. Blueboy actually looked ill at the prospect of losing all his hard-earned cash, we had no choice but to accept the situation and return home empty-handed.

I must add that Moiser was an excellent paymaster and had the venture been successful, Ron and I would have been well rewarded. Sad to say Blueboy has since passed away, but I'll wager you wherever he is, be it up or down, he'll be scheming to earn himself a few quid.

The Geoff Allen affair did have a happy ending as I decided to turn disadvantage to advantage and contact the man again. A few weeks later, I caught a train to

Bishop's Stortford, then travelled to Smith's Green by taxi. I approached the door of number 11, without a hint of trepidation and knocked. Geoff Allen opened the door and as I reintroduced myself, he interrupted and said he recalled my face from my previous visit to the abode. I told him I felt no malice towards him for what had happened and he said likewise, preferring to discount the incident. He seemed to admire my nerve and as we shook hands, he invited me into his cottage to discuss the possibility of doing some future business together. Since those days, Geoff has become a big property dealer, having owned and sold many mansions. Ron and I have been privileged to have guested at all of them until our internment.

A Pull In

When we were in our early twenties, Ron and I started to steal lorries for the loads they contained, irrespective of what it may be. During these daring ventures, we acquired consignments of furniture, sacks, fruit and whatever else we could manage to purloin. Once we had stolen the vehicle, we'd drive it to a remote farm to unload it and receive payment. Our three accomplices on these trips were: Dickie Mountain, Ron Bennett and Dickie Morgan.

On one occasion, we had stolen a load of fruit and were returning to the farm to unload it. Bearing in mind this was no Sunday outing, you can appreciate the speed at which we were travelling along the narrow country lanes, we certainly weren't adhering to any mandatory limits! Suddenly, as we approached a particularly bad bend, the driver who had failed to reduce his speed sufficiently enough to get round it, slammed on the brakes. The result was disaster. Half a load of Granny Smiths blocked the road, while the other half rolled away leading a trail to our lair. We cursed our luck but had little choice but to retrieve and reload the apples. That was one night when we certainly earned our money.

The night we stole the lorry of sacks and unloaded them was equally as laborious as retrieving the apples. The sacking was extremely coarse and after a night unloading my hands were covered in blisters. In spite of this, I loved the ambience of these night-time manoeuvres, especially in the early hours when day was breaking and the dew on the grass slithered like streaming tears. We stole so many loads that the East End tabloids reported that a black market gang was operating in the area.

The farmer who bought the stolen merchandise from us contacted us one day and put a fresh proposal our way. He needed a gang to take a lorry to the nearby air base and steal some aeroplane parts. He didn't need the parts for any particular usage, they were valuable for their metal content which was rather precious. The only drawback was that they were strewn around the airfield which was guarded by American Red Caps who were armed. Still, that did not deter us and although we dodged behind the lorry several times to avoid being detected, we successfully accomplished the mission on the farmer's behalf.

Dickie Morgan, one of the aforementioned accomplices in the lorry-stealing business, worked as an informer for the police against us during the trials of 1968. As well as stealing the lorry loads with us, Morgan has also served time with me in army detention, so his course of action was incomprehensible. I regard people with Morgan's morals as vermin, they are nothing more than sewer rats.

Billy Gentry

In 1965 Ron and I owned the El Morocco Club in Gerrard Street, Soho, but we eventually sold it to our friend, Billy Gentry alias Billy G. Billy Gentry is known to all the criminal fraternity throughout England and as I write this he is just beginning a ten-year sentence for conspiracy to rob. Billy looked after ex-cons for years, and probably would have made a good profession as a welfare officer had he not had criminal tendencies himself.

Billy was such a magnanimous character and when he took control of the El Morocco Club he would invite half the ex-prison population in the area to wine and dine at his expense. I remember we both had mini cars, although Billy's was a souped-up version, and we'd race each other from pub to pub on the occasions we went drinking together. Billy G is one of the old school of which I am sad to say there aren't many about nowadays. He is one character that I would dearly love to meet again on my travels; to shake his hand and thank him for years of loyalty towards Ron and I.

Tony Baldessaro

Although I had served time with Tony Baldessaro in Parkhurst, I had met him previously. In 1959, we were reunited once again in Wandsworth Prison. Tony was a bit of a lone wolf and really loathed prison. His face always showed a serious expression and he was adamant that this would be his last sentence; he'd never cross the threshold of a prison again. After serving twelve years, Tony was released to start his life anew. One day I picked up the daily paper and read to my dismay, how Tony Baldessaro had blown his brains out. He'd been absolute in his decision not to serve another jail term and when faced with the dilemma of returning to prison or suicide, he chose the latter. Over a period of time, he had committed several robberies and acquired a great deal of money from them which he accumulated. On the day of his death, the police surrounded his home and after an exchange of gunfire from both sides, Tony Baldessaro shot himself. The money which he had amassed from the robberies was found in the room, burnt to ashes.

Slip Sullivan

Slip Sullivan came from Finsbury Park and worked as a minder to a character by the name of Jack Jypp. Jypp was always in Spitalfields fruit market buying lorry loads of fruit and Sullivan would always accompany him to deter any would-be thieves who fancied their chances at purloining the large wad of notes Jypp always carried about his person. This union was beneficial to both men; Jypp because he liked the prestige associated to having a minder and Sullivan because Jack Jypp was a good paymaster to him. Slip Sullivan was also on Billy Hill's firm and when Tommy Smithson accosted Slip and slashed his face, Billy retaliated. Slip Sullivan along with Billy Hill and a few others, lured Tommy Smithson to a meeting and convinced him to hand over his gun, feigning an unwillingness to hostilities. When they had possession of the gun, they smashed him over the head with an iron bar and almost amputated Smithson's arm with a razor.

Throughout his whole life, Slip Sullivan had been involved in countless feuds and gangland warfare but survived the ordeals practically unscathed, so it is ironic that his life ended when a woman plunged a knife into him as they lay in bed. When I heard about this I recalled Old Dodger Mullins telling me 'never trust a woman, they could be dangerous and could stick a glass in your face as any man could'.

George Sewell

George Sewell from Tottenham was one of the nicest fellas I ever met. He was of similar age to my father, extremely handsome and built like a tank. George had two famous sons George Junior, the television and film actor, and Danny who was a heavyweight fighter. Danny fought twenty-two fights without defeat and was well on the way to reaching the top when he contracted polio and was forced to retire. His father, George, sent him to America to help him recuperate and when he overcame his illness, Danny moved into films and became a successful actor in Western pictures. To my knowledge he is still in the States today.

As I write this, I am unable to say if George Sewell is still alive or not, but either way I am sure he would have no objection to me writing this story about him. He was never a villain in the sense that he earned money from crime, he was always a straight man reaping his living in an honest way. However, I feel it necessary to include him in this book of 'villains' because most of London's tearaways steered well clear of George Sewell. Although he was as straight as a die, George was recognized all over London as a fighting man. His fists were like iron bars and cut off all the bare-knuckle fights he competed in on the cobblestones. He never lost one. Sad to say, George was the victim of a razor slashing, which resulted in a terrible scar running deep down the right-hand side of his face.

Big Jimmy Kensit

Jimmy Kensit was big proud fighting man and if he were alive today, he'd be even prouder by the success of his grandchildren, Patsy and Jamie. Patsy has achieved international fame as a film actress, starring in such films as 'Lethal Weapon 2' with Mel Gibson, and Jamie formed his own pop group. The group proved to be highly successful in the eighties when they had a huge hit with Patsy fronting the band and singing lead vocals.

Big Jimmy came from Shoreditch in the Hoxton area, and was a big friend of my paternal grandfather, Jimmy Kray. They had many a tough battle, fighting together as allies, side-by-side around the streets of Hoxton. Big Jim's son, Jimmy Kensit grew up to be a professional featherweight fighter and was also one of the best money-earners I have ever come across. I was deeply honoured when Jimmy Junior and his wife asked me to be godfather to their son, Jamie, and I have fond memories of the christening ceremony and celebrations afterwards. Jimmy's wife was one of the most charming women I have ever met and always made me welcome into their home. It is easy to see where her daughter Patsy got her looks from, having such an attractive mother.

One night I was in the Green Dragon Gambling Club and as the evening wore on, one punter began to get very vociferous and directed his attention my way. I must have been on a short fuse that night, for I hit him on the chin and knocked him in the air with a left hook then escorted him off the premises. A few days later, the news filtered through that the fella's brother was trying to buy a gun with the intention of shooting me. I threw a few ideas around in my head over what I should do until the perfect scheme came to mind, and I immediately began to put it into action. I managed to obtain a gun and had it altered so that when it was used it would backfire and blow off, or very seriously injure the hand squeezing the trigger. I contacted an old friend, Kenny Medleycott who I had been in Wandsworth Prison with in 1959 and said I required his services. I gave him sufficient money and the gun, and told him to go to a drinking club in Bow that was run by a coloured fella. When he arrived there, he was to seek out and join the company of the brother wishing to purchase a gun and sell the fixed weapon to him. Medleycott carried out my plan to perfection and sold the gun as instructed. As it happened, the brother never did carry out his threat but had he done so he would have been perfectly armless!

Sometimes I like and enjoy complex thinking rather than just the straightforward way and this was just one of those times.

Chopper Watts

Chopper Watts from Walthamstow is another old villain I have fond memories of. He was a regular customer to our gambling club in that area called the Stow Club. His nickname was attributed to him for the obvious reason; he always had a hatchet concealed about his person.

Willie and Charlie Malone

Two of the best street fighters in London came from Stepney in the East End. They were the Malone brothers, the eldest being Willie, and Charlie the younger of the two. Willie had a massive pair of shoulders which supported an equally huge bull neck. They had both been dockers in their teens and were hard-drinking men. For a time, they both worked with Ron and I. Charlie looked after the Green Dragon Social Club for us while Willie worked alongside Ron. These days they've both retired, but Willie owns his own tea company. Their relation, Jimmy Fullerton was also considered a fighting man but he sadly died in a car crash.

Billy Pinnock

Billy Pinnock was a North London pickpocket. After an argument with some rivals, he was thrown out of a speeding car and sustained a broken jaw. Although he was a friend of my father's, he would often educate Ron and I by teaching us the tricks of the trade.

Roy Shaw

Roy Shaw was an ex-professional fighter but altered his venue from the ring to the streets. Roy was convicted of robbery and served a fifteen-year prison term which included a short stint in Broadmoor Hospital. When he was released Roy took up professional street fighting. As I write this they are considering making a film of Roy's life.

Arthur Scully

Gypsy Arthur Scully came from Upton Park and was one of Jack Spot's firm in the early days. I never had the pleasure of meeting him because he sadly died at a young age from a disease; nevertheless I heard about his fighting exploits when he would smash his enemies around the face with a chain.

Another two from Upton Park were little Jacky Reynolds and Billy Robbins, also fighting men. One particular day, Teddy Machent smashed a drinking glass into the face of Jacky Reynolds. Needless to say Jack declined to prosecute Machent. He even had the offer of outside help when people hearing about the attack phoned him, but he refused all offers saying he would even the score himself.

There was Nicky Carter, the villain from Paddington and also Jimmy Smith from the same area who could pack a punch like Rocky Marciano. Dave Barry, the good money-earner was from Paddington too. On one occasion he served four years for taking part in a smash-and-grab raid. Dave was also a capable fighter and was convicted of manslaughter when a punch he threw on a fella's chin killed him. There was also the tough Mike Connors from Holborn who knew everyone in London. I also recall Ginger Dennis, another face who was given four years for the attack on Jack Spot.

My old man was always telling stories about his friend, Charlie Barwick. Charlie was born in Hackney and according to my father, he had the best left hook he'd ever seen. He became very adept at knocking out policemen with his left hook and really shaped up well. He had been to prison on several occasions and I'm sad to say that one of his sentences was never completed. Charlie Barwick died in Liverpool Prison of kidney trouble although what caused the ailment remains a mystery.

There were also fringe men who mixed with all the villains. Two I can recollect were Sulky and Al Burnett. Sulky was the manager of the Astor Club and he always wore a red carnation in his lapel. Al Burnett managed the Stork Club in Swallow Street. Both were two of London's most famous characters. Al Burnett at one time owned the racing greyhound 'Pigalle Wonder' which was named after one of his other clubs 'Pigalle', off Regent Street. Al Burnett entered the literary world by writing a book 'Ace of Clubs' which referred to and contained details of his involvement in the Clubland. He certainly encountered plenty of stars in the fifties and sixties and was an amiable host to all.

Jimmy Nash

The Pen Club was a favourite East End haunt for many villains. It was situated in an upstairs building in the vicinity of Spitalfields Market. During the early hours the patrons would start to drift in with the assurance that genial company and a relaxed atmosphere awaited them. It wasn't renowned for being a trouble spot, in fact quite the opposite, which accounted for its popularity at this hour of the day.

During the early hours of one particular drinking session, an altercation started between the club owners, Jimmy Cooney and Billy Ambrose and some customers who were not proven members. They were led by Jimmy Nash who had seven brothers including John Nash who I have previously mentioned. Jimmy Nash was a well-known figure in the London underworld and had a certain reputation. He was of strong build with a thick bull neck and sported a short, cropped, crew-cut hairstyle. He had a fetish for collecting any memorabilia connected with Germans or Germany and was an avid reader of torture books. After finishing the stories, he got great satisfaction in reciting extracts from them, particularly the worst bits which contained all the gory details.

Others in his party that night were Joe Pyle and John Reed. Reed was the son of a Croydon policeman and like Pyle, had once been a professional fighter. Billy Ambrose was well-known as an ex-middleweight professional fighter and at the time, he was on parole after serving a prison sentence at Dartmoor. He'd been convicted to serve a term of eleven years for stealing a large quantity of gold pens from a warehouse which explains why 'The Pen Club' was so named.

In the early days of his sentence, Ambrose had been admitted to the hospital wing at Wormwood Scrubs where he seized the opportunity to escape. Unfortunately, his freedom was shortlived. He was eventually recaptured and sent to the Moor where he remained until his parole. On the night of the argument, Cooney and Ambrose advanced towards Nash to try calm the situation down and prevent any further incident. The prosecution alleged that Nash removed from his coat pocket a German Mauser and fired, point-blank without warning at the approaching men. Jimmy Cooney was hit in the chest and Billy Ambrose caught it in the stomach. Cooney staggered down the stairs to the dimly-lit street, blood gushing from the wound in his chest trying to seek sanctuary, when his balance gave way and he keeled over to fall in the gutter. His girlfriend, Fay Sadler rushed to console him and cradled his head close to her body as though he were resting in the arms of Morpheus. Sad to say the shot proved to be fatal and Jimmy Cooper died where he lay. Billy Ambrose had the presence of mind to jump in his car and drive to the London Hospital where emergency surgery saved his life. The fact that Ambrose had kept his body in peak condition and was extremely fit and healthy probably contributed to his recovery.

After the fatal shooting, Jimmy Nash, Joe Pyle and John Reed left the Pen Club and headed straight for my mother's house which was close by, to seek assistance from Ron and I. They told us they were in a bit of trouble, but this was the understatement of the year! Jimmy Cooney had once managed a drinking club for Aggie Hill, the wife of Billy Hill, before they divorced, so we were familiar with Cooney and his girlfriend Fay Sadler. Also, Ron and I had always had a good relationship with Billy Ambrose, beginning when we trained together at Bill Cline's gym in Great Portland Street. Billy was an exceptional fighter and a man of good principles and I felt I could reason with him. My decision to pay Bill a visit at the London hospital was for two reasons. One was out of respect and the other to find out information. I needed to be clued up on how many witnesses were present on the night in question, so they could be intercepted and asked not to give evidence against the three accused men; Nash, Pyle and Reed. Just before I entered the hospital ward, I surreptitiously looked around the corridor to see who was present. I noticed a woman, who I recognized as Billy's wife, Jerry Callaghan, a close friend of Bill's and other personal friends but thankfully no law. Jerry and I acknowledged each other by a nodding gesture as I politely asked Bill's wife for permission to visit her husband for five minutes, for which she nodded affirmatively. I was in a bit of a dilemma with the assignment I had undertaken. I had the utmost respect for Billy Ambrose, which he knew, and being a man of such good conduct I was certain he wouldn't deviate from the moral code he'd always believed in and upheld, and prosecute Nash and the others. Billy himself was man enough to appreciate and accept the situation I was in; pleading leniency on the accused's behalf to their victim, but he didn't take it as a personal slight against him and knowing this eased my conscience.

The night prior to the Pen Club shootings, I had been drinking in the Green Dragon Social Club which was run by Sonny the Yank, one of Jack Spot's ex-firm members. I was in conversation with the Yank and another fella, when the Yank called me 'son' in what I felt a derogatory manner. As I rose to put on my overcoat and kid gloves to leave, he reiterated the same phrase in the exact condescending way. I turned and hit the Yank on the point of his chin with a right hook which lifted him three feet in the air. As he was falling, I grabbed him by the shirt collar and butted him in the face which was quite unnecessary as the first punch had knocked him out cold and broken his jaw. Ron and I later took control of the Green Dragon Social Club. The next day when I visited Billy Ambrose in hospital, I observed the opposite side of the ward and three beds away, Sonny the Yank was propped up in bed with his gaping jaw!

Jimmy, Joe and John were eventually arrested and

charged with murder. The trial was to take place at the Old Bailey. While the trial was pending, Ron and I visited Jimmy Nash who was on remand in the hospital section of Brixton Prison. It was normal practice to admit murderers onto the hospital wing. A screw sat close to Jimmy whilst we spoke and took notes to record the conversation. Jimmy was not at all intimidated or perturbed by the officer's presence, and as we continued to speak, he made a noose out of a thread of cotton and dangled it to and fro. Jimmy always did have a bizarre sense of humour and this little joke seemed to please him immensely. I had made a point of meeting all the witnesses to the shooting and invited them to the Double R Club for drinks. As I sat drinking with Fay Sadler, Jimmy Cooney's girlfriend, she intimated that she would disappear for a while in exchange for a favour. Apparently she had some medical problems and required the immediate services of a good doctor. Fortunately, we had an excellent doctor on the firm and a compromise was reached.

During the trial, I sat with Jimmy Nash in the part of the court set aside for the accused's family. I watched the jury intently trying to contemplate their thoughts, when I was distracted and aware of Chief Inspector Vibart of Scotland Yard observing me. Jimmy Nash's barrister was a man called Victor Durand. Jimmy Nash was found guilty of manslaughter and sentenced to five years' imprisonment, Joe Pyle and John Reed were both acquitted. Ron and I were with the other members of our firm sitting in a gambling club at Wellington Way, Bow, in the East End of London, when the news bulletin giving the verdict was transmitted. We were all ecstatic at the end result and raised our glasses to Jimmy, Joe and John.

We also toasted the health of Billy Ambrose who not only refused to testify against the accused, but actually helped them in their defence. Today Billy Ambrose is a highly successful businessman, in the high bracket income class but in the opinions of Ron and I he deserves everything he's got because it couldn't have happened to a nicer fella.

Bobby Ramsey

Bobby Ramsey was an ex-professional lightweight fighter. He was handsome in looks despite his typical pugilistic nose. Bobby generally wore a smart cashmere overcoat with accessories like kid gloves and a hat to complement his style. After his retirement from the ring, Bobby accompanied Billy Hill to Johannesburg in South Africa as his minder. As this story has already been reported in the Billy Hill chapter, I don't think it's necessary to recount all the details except to remind the reader that Bobby was sentenced to three months' imprisonment.

On his return to England, Bobby went to work, (I use the word lightly) for Jack Spot the gangland boss. Ron and I first met Ramsey during our early teens and he influenced our lifestyles, character and attitudes. Bobby was a proud owner of a maroon-coloured Buick and could often be seen flying around the streets of London as if there was no tomorrow. He was one of the most interesting and illuminating personalities around and would stand up to anyone on the cobbles.

left to right: Ron Hart, Ritchi Anderson, Ron Kray, a friend & Sam Ledaman

left to right: Lou Bercovitch, his wife, Scotty Sheppard, Harry Sheppard

left to right: Pat Connelly, Billy Kray, Jim Harris, Charles Kray Snr., Billy Conn

left to right: Kicki Mountain, third from left: Duke Osbourne, Ronnie Ward, Teddy Smith, Ron Kray, Big Pat Connelly, Charlie Malone & Reg Kray

Ronnie & Reg Kray at home at Vallance Road

Jimmy Nash

Right: Duke Osbourne, Ron, Maxi Rosenbloom, Reg & Tommy Brown

Below: Pat Connelly, Terry Spinks & Ron Kray

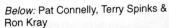

Jimmy Boyle

Pat Connelly &
Limehouse Willy

Ronnie Kray &
Battles Rossi

Shaw

George Woods

Below: Back Row, left to
right: Pat Butler, George
Osbourne, Reg Kray,
Ron Kray, Terry Dean
Front: Ronald Stafford,
Teddy Smith, Charlie Kray,
Tommy Yeardy &
Limehouse Willy

George Carpentier, Ronnie
Kray & friend

Pat Connelly, George Sewell &
wife, Barbara Windsor

left to right: Bulla Ward, Fred Foreman, Charlie Kray,
Albert Donogue, Billy Donovan, Reg Kray,
Dickie Mountain, Terry Allen Ron Kray,
Red Faced Tommy, Fat Staff, Pat Connelly,
George Osbourne, Harry, front: Fred Cavagner,
Eddie Flowers, Charles Kray Snr, & Mick Forsyth.

Charles Kray, Reg Kray, Terry Allen, Ron Kray,
Barney Beal, Freddie Foreman & Buster Edwards.

Left: left to right: Tony Snyder, Charlie Kray, Georgie Woods, Ron Kray

Below left : Sulky, Matt Wells, Barney Beal, Kid Burges, Charlie Kray & Billy Hill

Below: Reg's wife, Francis, Billy Colouleus & Reg

Left: left to right: Patrick Kennedy, second from right: Broderick Crawford, none of these are villians

Right: Ronnie Kray, Ted Kid Lewis & Sophie Tucker

Left: Ron, Victor Spinetti, Tom Driberg, Tommy Brown, Charlie Kray, Deve Simms, Reg Kray, Ted Kid Lewis, Len Harvey, Terry Spinks & Steve Clark

Below: Red Faced Tommy, Ted Kid Burges & Ronnie Kray

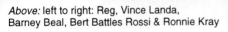

Above: left to right: Reg, Vince Landa, Barney Beal, Bert Battles Rossi & Ronnie Kray

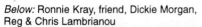

Below: Ronnie Kray, friend, Dickie Morgan, Reg & Chris Lambrianou

Billy Daniels

Terry Spinks, Ron Kray, Bobby
Ramsey & Sonny Liston

Henry Simmonds, Reg Kray,
Bobby Ramsey, Sonny Liston,
Reg Kray & Harry Collins

Connie Whitehead, Pat
Connolly, Rocky Marciano,
Alex Stein, George Raft

Ted Kid Burgess, Ted Kid Lewis &
Terry Spinks

Joe Louis, Micky Morris, Ron
Kray & friends

Ron Kray & Billy Walker

Ian Barrie & Reg Kray

Terry Allen, Ronnie Kray &
Charles Kray Snr.

Sam McCarthy, Charlie Kray,
Buster Oborne & Fred Foreman

Reg, Bulla Ward, Bert Rossi,
Red-Faced Tommy & Ron

Frank Sinatra Jnr.,

Pat Connelly, William Frost, Mrs Pat
Whitehead, Connie Whitehead, Rag Kray &
Francis Kray

Charlie Kray, Ron Kray &
Eddie Pucci

Micky Forsyth, Billy Daniels, Reg, Squibbie, Eric Mason & Ron Kray

Above: Salvatore Messina

Left: Maxi Rosenbloom

Below left: Maxi Rosenbloom, Duke Owney Madden, George Raft & Kid Francis

Ron, Billy Conn, & Reg

Above: Anthony 'Tony Ducks' Corallo

Angleo Bruno

Below: Guys & Dolls: Betty Grable, Dan Dailey, Alan Gale, Lola Fisher & Maxi Rosenbloom

Ron & Reg Kray

Eddie Pucci, Ron Kray, Goerge Raft, Reg Kray & Rocky Marciano

Eddie Pucci, Rocky Marciano & George Raft

Dickie Morgan, Willy Pep, Ron Kray & Alan Cooper

Ronnie Kray in New York with Joe Kaufman

Ronnie & Billy Conn

THE DOUBLE R R CLUB

145, BOW ROAD, E.3.

OPEN   SUNDAY
3 – 11 p.m.   1 – 3 p.m.
                    7 – 10 p.m.

8 9

Signature...

Directors: The Right Honourable The Earl of Effingham
R. Kray, L. Payne, R. Kray, C. Kray, A. Kray.

ESMERALDA'S BARN LTD.

50, Wilton Place,
Knightsbridge,
London, S.W.1.   Telephone:
                                  BELgravia 3040/3039

THE DOUBLE R R CLUB

Proprietors R.R.&C. KRAY

MODERN BAR   —   MUSIC EVERY NIGHT

Open 3–11pm weekdays 1–3pm & 7–10pm Sundays

145 BOW RD. LONDON E.3.

Patsy Manning Co-author with Reg in 'Reg Kray's Book of Slang'

On one occasion, the slag George Ince pulled a flick knife on Bobby and threatened to slash him. This did not deter Ramsey. He swiftly disarmed the low-life rat and with a single punch knocked him out cold.

In Victoria Park, there was a boxing booth where fighters would challenge opponents to try their luck in the ring for a wager. A friend of ours accepted the challenge and entered the ring. His name was Ronnie Sorrall and he was outclassed in every way by his opponent who towered head and shoulders above him. Everyone anticipated that the fighter would take it easy with Ronnie as he knew he had the edge over him but he treated him unmercifully and the contest ended with Ronnie knocked out. This unethical display of brutality enraged and provoked me so much that I decided to give the fighter a taste of his own medicine. I contacted Bobby Ramsey and asked him to accept the challenge and compete against the booth fighter to ensure he'd never take liberties again. We drove to the venue in two cars and Bobby was accepted by the fighter who was totally unaware of what fate had in store for him. Bobby fought as though it were a professional bout and watching him in action was like a flashback to his early days in the ring. To give credit where it's due, the fighter was game, but no match for Bobby who knocked him through the ropes to a resounding victory. As a professional fighter, Bobby Ramsey fought Danny Webb, the coloured Canadian Empire Champion. During the bout Ramsey spat in Webb's face, then they gouged each other with their thumbs and set to, butting each other like billy-goats. Ramsey eventually won the fight on points; his best victory in the ring and it was considered to be the fight amongst fights by those who watched it.

Ron and I, along with Billy Jones and Bobby Ramsey, were all charged with malicious wounding against Terry Martin and sent to the Old Bailey for trial. I was acquitted but Ron and Billy Jones received three years and Bobby Ramsey was sentenced to seven.

Ramsey served his time in Dartmoor and Wakefield prisons. He had an operation to straighten his nose and went into films as a bit-part actor. Whenever I catch a glimpse of his face on the small screen, I think back to his wilder days when he first knocked on our door at Vallance Road saying Charlie had sent him to see us.

The Cat Burglar: Charlie Clark

One day when I was reading through my daily deluge of post at Gartree Prison, I came across a missive from an old friend of Ron and I, Charlie Bateman, alias Charlie Clark who had died aged seventy-one. Also in the letter was a press cutting from a Kent newspaper which read: MURDER – REMAND, a Dover man appeared in court on Monday charged with murdering a disabled pensioner. Shane Keeler 18, unemployed is accused of murdering Charlie Bateman, 71, who was found dead at his Dover home on Friday. Keeler was remanded in custody until the following Wednesday.

What the write-up failed to mention was that during the fifties and sixties, Charlie Clark was one of the best cat burglars in London. He was always in the company of Ron and I and the rest of the firm, when we went out to wine and dine each night. Charlie Bateman was about six feet tall and to me, had looks synonymous with Gary Cooper as well as the mannerisms. At seventy-one, I should imagine his facial features would have altered a lot and the young perpetrator Shane Keeler wouldn't have had a clue as to Charlie Bateman's real identity.

Charlie Clark and his wife Sylvia had a bungalow in Chingford and they would lend it out to use it for meetings and holding parties. They both had a passion for cats and the bungalow was never empty of felines, but the place was always spotlessly clean. Charlie was also a compulsive gambler and always had a twinkle in his blue eyes as though he found everything amusing. At this moment in time, I don't know the details or reasons why he was found dead in his home, but I'll wager you, if he could, he'd give Shane Keeler any help he could to prevent him being prosecuted and he'd do it with a twinkle in his eyes.

Charlie Clark's favourite of favourites was my brother Ron. He was a regular visitor to Broadmoor despite his advancing years and wrote without fail every week. It's been said that Charlie was the best climber in the business and that's how and why he became known as 'The Cat Man'. The Cat Man had moved away from London preferring to spend his twilight years in the peace and tranquillity of his Kent home. This wish was to be denied him. The violence of the concrete jungle that he had gone out of his way to avoid, followed him to the 'Garden of England'. This surely would have brought a sparkle to the eyes of the Cat Man as the irony of it all would have amused him so much.

Harry Sheppard

Harry Sheppard was born in Aldgate in the East End of London. For many years he was a permanent resident in the city of Montreal, Canada, where he was recognized as one of the top boxing figures. Harry was extradited from the country when he was involved in a national public scandal. The Canadian authorities had arrested him in connection with the shooting and the death of one Billy Davies. Lou Bercovitch, the Montreal gangster, was responsible for shooting Davies as he sat behind his desk working. Bercovitch was arrested and sentenced to life imprisonment while Sheppard was deported back to London.

Ron and I first met Harry Sheppard in the Vienna Rooms in Edgware Road, when we were in our twenties. Harry became like a father-figure to us and we would sit rapt for hours while he told us fascinating stories about his life; of times when he and his wife, Scotty, would wine and dine with Dean Martin and many other celebrities. For years Harry had mixed with top Mafia figures and the gangsters in Canada, New York and London held him in the highest regard. Harry always wore a smart snap-brim hat and was an impeccable dresser. His wife, Scotty was a marvellous woman and Harry first introduced us to her at the Grave Maurice public house.

Harry Sheppard used to manage some of the world's greatest fighters such as Gordon Wallace and Ynon Durelle, as well as many others. Durelle fought Archie Moore for the light heavyweight Championship of the World at the Forum in Montreal in 1958. Durelle floored him four times, three times in the first round, but Moore staggered back to dish out the same treatment and retain his crown. Gordon Wallace beat our own Ron Barton. Harry arranged for Ron and I to meet Durelle and Wallace in their rooms at the Cumberland Hotel before they fought in London. Ron and I would sit for hours listening to Harry speaking about Lou Bercovitch in the Vienna Rooms. His Canadian accent seemed to add more impetus to the stories.

Lou was finally released after serving eleven years of his life sentence but died of a heart attack a few years later. Harry Sheppard died before Ron and I were convicted and though Scotty wrote to us for many years, sadly she lost her sight and I have not heard from her for a long time.

When I sit and think of Harry Sheppard and Lou Bercovitch and the good lifestyle they lived before their ultimate end, I think of the Chinese proverb which tells of a passerby who walked by a dilapidated castle that had seen grander times. Then the passerby stopped at a mill pond nearby the castle and he spoke into the stillness of the pond and said, 'If I could ask you a question on time, what would the answer be?' and the stillness of the pond answered, 'A thousand years have passed by since yesterday!'

The Villains

My brother Ron and I were eighteen years of age and on the run from the Army, and one particular night were seated at a table having a meal of steak, chips and peas in Wallies Café, which was next door to the bus station, in the area of London Fields, Hackney, London. We and the other villains frequented this café and as we ate our meals, and had conversation, in walked through the café door, a fella about thirty years of age who was well dressed and walked with an agile step. His face had high cheekbones, a slightly broken nose and brown eyes, he was about five feet nine inches tall and weighed about thirteen stone. With him were two other men and a couple of women.

On his entrance all the conversation seemed to stop at once and all eyes looked towards the group of arrivals. The quietness seemed to be a silent tribute of unspoken respect to this leader of the group, and if one listened carefully, one could pick up a whisper from those at the tables saying to those who did not know, that it was Tommy Smithson. Tommy Smithson was liked and respected by all the young villains in the area of London Fields, Hackney and also all over London. He had built up a reputation as a villain, a gambler and a fighting man; he was in fact the villain's villain, and had become a legend and part of the folklore in the rough circles of London.

Tommy was born in the area of Hackney, London, and had for some time been a merchant seaman. Since then he had run the Crown and Anchor boards in the area which got him a living but was only part of the way he made money. Crown and Anchor boards were used for card games where the punters would place a bet on a card and try to win a few quid, but the board men like Tommy Smithson hardly ever lost to the punter. At one time Tommy Smithson had fought a battle against big Alf Melvin and Alf had struck Tommy in the head with a machete but Tommy fought on. Another time Tommy had a knuckle fight with the best of all the fighters on the cobbles, Jimmy Spinks. These and other battles were part of what made Tommy Smithson a living legend, and he had also done some booth fighting. He was to all the young villains a man they would like to be and he used to drive around in a black American Buick, which seemed to suit his lifestyle and image. Ron and I were proud to be on talking terms with Smithson, and at one time when we had trouble with a firm from Edmonton, he offered us his help but we respectfully declined the offer.

During this time Lyons Corner House, in Tottenham Court Road, was open until the early hours of the morning, and all the villains and prostitutes from all over London would frequent the place. I often saw Tommy Smithson give money to down-and-out women of the street, and these women thought the world of Tommy; his generosity was an example to those who looked on.

At one time Tommy had cut one of Billy Hill's firm, so Billy and the other members of his firm made a meet with Tommy Smithson to talk things over. At this particular time Smithson, who was basically a loner, was armed with a revolver and the meet had been arranged in a back street, off Edgware Road. Tommy and the group stood talking near the parked cars and Moiser Blueboy kidded to Tommy to hand over the revolver to him. Moiser said that they should all be friends but as soon as Tommy gave the shooters over he was struck on the head from behind. Billy Hill and the others mutilated his arm, as he lay unconscious, almost cutting the arm off. He was later put into a car, and the assailants drove to Hyde Park where they dumped the unconscious Tommy Smithson. This attack was a reprisal because Tommy had cut Slip Sullivan. When Tommy was at the hospital, Billy Hill sent a messenger to see Tommy to keep him sweet so that he would not prosecute. The messenger gave Tommy an envelope which contained £500, but Tommy true to his code took one glance at the money and handed it back to the messenger saying, 'Don't insult me, you know I won't pros.' When Tommy used the word 'pros' it was short for prosecute. This time was around the 1950s and £500 was a considerable sum.

Some time later Tommy had a row with Tony Mulla, and Tony slashed Tommy's face badly with a knife, but Tommy was not always on the losing end. One night, myself and Ron had nowhere to sleep, had no money and were on the run from the Army. We were in the Lyons Corner House where Tommy Smithson was having a cup of strong black coffee, and he sussed that we were skint and had nowhere to sleep. At this time he had a speil off Barwick Street, Soho and Tommy gave us a couple of quid and the keys to the speil. He said we could stay there overnight but we were to leave at 8.00 a.m. in the morning. He told us where to leave the keys and said that we could use the tea and coffee from behind the bar. The speil also had in it one large billiard table where Ron and I slept on this particular night.

Three or four years later, Tommy Smithson got into an argument with some Maltese people in an East End speil off Commercial Road. A couple of days after the argument Tommy went to see these two Maltese people who lived in a flat in the Bayswater area. When he met them another argument started and one of the Maltese pulled out a small revolver and shot Tommy in the neck. Another bullet went through his right arm, but Tommy was so game that this did not stop him. He chased the two Maltese down the stairs of the flat, onto the pavement outside but then Tommy collapsed in a pool of blood and died.

Tommy died at thirty-four years of age. The two Maltese went on trial for murder, and claimed that Tommy was demanding money from them. One of them was acquitted, and the other one by the name of Elul was given a life sentence of which he served eleven years. He now lives in the United States.

My brother Ron and I were present at Tommy Smithson's funeral, and just prior to the funeral procession we entered the little terraced house where Tommy lay in an open coffin and we took a last look at him and paid our silent respects. He looked at peace, and I noticed that the bullet hole in his neck had been plugged by the mortician with cotton wool. Villains from all over London came to pay their respects, and one of these was Steve Murphy, who I have already mentioned as being one of our best friends. There were wreaths of all shapes and sizes placed on top of the cars, of which there were many in a long convoy. There was one wreath in the shape of a boxing ring, and another in the shape of a pair of dice showing snake's eyes to depict that Tommy's luck had run out.

The Mayfair Playboy

Peter Jenkins was known as the 'Mayfair Playboy'. He had been convicted of a jewellery robbery in the 1950s which took place in a hotel in the Mayfair area. Peter Jenkins and his accomplice both booked into a Mayfair Hotel and they phoned a jeweller and asked the manager of the shop to bring a tray of valuable rings in a briefcase at a specified time. He took the tray of rings out and displayed them on the table in the hotel room so that Peter Jenkins and his accomplice could look and select an engagement ring. Peter Jenkins and his accomplice were both booked into the hotel under aliases and false addresses. They had planned this robbery for some time and when the jeweller placed the jewellery on the table they did not hesitate to bludgeon him around his head with coshes and he fell to the floor with blood gushing from his head wounds. They picked up the jewellery and placed the tray in a small case and left the hotel. Sometime later Peter Jenkins, known as the Mayfair Playboy was arrested with his colleague and charged with malicious wounding and robbery. They had been spending the proceeds in various nightclubs in such a way that they had drawn attention to themselves.

When Peter Jenkins appeared at the Old Bailey in the number one court, the gallery was packed with débutantes and society people. They had come to see their fallen society member even though he was disgraced. Jenkins and his co-accused were sentenced to seven years' penal servitude. Peter Jenkins was sent to Dartmoor Prison to serve his sentence. Ron and I were looking after him with tobacco and the odd bottle of scotch while he stayed at Dartmoor and when he was eventually released he came to the Double R Club which Ron and I ran at the time. I greeted Peter Jenkins and I could not help feeling sorry for him because the sentence had taken its toll on him and I weighed him up as the non-criminal type. Despite the fact that he had just come out of prison, he was obviously in the strange alien world of the criminal society which had been forced upon him when he received his seven-year sentence.

The Double R Club was frequented by the criminal types as well as straight people and when Peter Jenkins was in conversation with some of the criminal element in the club I could see he was like a fish out of water. It was obvious to me that it must have been the same for him when he was in Dartmoor Prison, so much more of an ordeal when he was serving his sentence. He was now an alcoholic and all he had left was his educated way of speaking and his gentlemanly ways.

I guess if one had put a Dartmoor convict to live in an area of society people it would have been a similar extreme to what the Mayfair Playboy had to undergo in such a hostile environment as that of Dartmoor Prison. I gave Peter Jenkins a few quid and made his night as comfortable as possible and plied him with drinks.

Some years later I read a daily newspaper which had a very small write-up in it that read Peter Jenkins alias the Mayfair Playboy had been found dead in a lodging house in the area of Bayswater. He had died of alcohol poisoning. It seemed that Peter Jenkins could never pick up the pieces to start a new life and had been banished from the life of high society since his conviction – he didn't have the knowledge to make it in the underworld which was so alien to him. I found

Peter Jenkins an interesting but sad victim of life's stage.

The Money Getters

When I think of good money getters, four names come to mind right away from the 1950s and 1960s. One of these was Dave Barry who came from Paddington. He had a small club off Church Street in Paddington, and my brother Ron, Billy Jones and myself would visit this small drinking club regularly. We would discuss different ways to earn money with the club owner, Dave, who was always keen to earn a few quid. Dave was one of the best money getters in London. At one time many years ago, as I have said earlier in my book, Dave had been given a sentence of four years for a smash-and-grab robbery on a fur shop, and another time he was given an eighteen-month sentence for manslaughter. Dave was related to a famous cricketer.

Another money getter who used to use all the exclusive clubs for gambling was Tony S. He used to play cards until the early hours, and he dressed like a film star. At one time he earned money by helping to bring plane-loads of people to this country, from America to play cards at the well-known casinos. These trips were called junkets, and Tony was good at organizing them. In recent years I have been told that Tony is very wealthy. My feelings on this are good luck to him.

Tommy Falco from Clerkenwell used to be one of those in charge of the point-to-point races. He would allocate the bookmakers' pitches, to those who paid for the privilege of making a book, so that punters could place bets during the different races. Tommy and his family were good friends of Ron and I. Tommy died some time ago.

The last one out of these four was Bobby from West London. He was, and probably still is, one of the real top money-earners, and at one time he had a villa in Tangier. Bob once got arrested for forgery of English currency notes, and he was given seven years at the end of his trial. The judge commented that the fraud was of such a large scale, the flooding of the money market by this forged currency could have changed the economy of the country.

When I think of gamblers and smart dressers, my mind thinks of Ginger Ted, who used to have a club in the Bayswater area which was open for twenty-four hour periods for those who gambled. Ted was one of the best card players in London, one of the smartest dressers, and he was very much a part of the 1950s and 1960s.

Colin Osbourne alias Duke Osbourne

Duke Osbourne was a friend of ours for many years. He came from Victoria in London, and was a villain and a thief. Duke was a good dresser, over six feet tall and had a slim build but he had a big heart when it came to being game when faced with any trouble. He was fanatical about arms, and in 1964 when Ron and I were on trial at the Old Bailey, Duke was also on trial on a different case in one of the other courts at the Old Bailey. Duke had been charged with being in the possession of a cache of arms that were found in his flat at Cambridge Heath Road in the East End. Duke was found guilty of this charge and was given a sentence of seven years. During his sentence, he had been in an argument in the TV room at Gartree Prison and had been badly stabbed, but he lived. When Duke was released he vowed never to go back to prison, and he visited Ron and myself at Parkhurst.

During the late fifties and early sixties, Duke was with us most of the time, and he used to enjoy the nightlife which we all led. He was known by all the criminal fraternity as Duke and was trusted by all. During my latter years at Parkhurst, I was watching the TV news when it was announced that London gangster, Duke Osbourne had been found dead in the area of Hackney Downs. I was sad at this news. My brother, Charlie, took care of Duke's funeral and an inquest left an open verdict on Duke's death.

In the London circles, it was said that Duke was wanted for serious questioning by the police, and so he decided to take his own life. I believe this rumour to be true. The Duke was sadly missed by all who knew him.

Eric Mason

Eric Mason used to host the Brown Derby in the West End. I first became friends with Eric in the early 1950s, and in 1959 we were both in Wandsworth

Prison. We found out who the sex cases were and we'd hit them on the chin.

At one time Eric had served a seven-year sentence in Dartmoor Prison, and during this sentence he had assaulted a screw. For his punishment he had been given so many strokes of the cat-o'-nine-tails. He was probably one of the last prisoners to be given the punishment of being whipped. During his stay at Dartmoor, he worked in a rock quarry, and during an argument in the quarry with another prisoner, he hit the prisoner with an iron bar and knocked the fella's teeth out.

Eric and a fella by the name of John Squibb, and myself, went to Stockholm in Sweden in 1963, to watch the Floyd Patterson – Eddie Machen fight and we stayed at the Grand Hotel. I always found Eric to be a sound person, and I learned recently that he is happily married with a family, and has written a manuscript which is called, 'Inside Story', which I am sure will be a success.

Joe Pyle

During the 1950s and 1960s, if one went to the Astor Club just off Berkeley Square, or to the Pigalle Restaurant in Regent Street, in the early hours of the morning, one would be sure to meet up with Joe Pyle who came from Morden in Surrey. Joe has always been an easygoing likeable person, and at times his good looks could deceive, because in his twenties he had been a good middleweight professional fighter. Joe has always been a good businessman, and a man of his word.

During the 1960s, he had been acquitted of murder during the Pen Club case, when Jimmy Nash had been found guilty of manslaughter and sentenced to five years in prison. Joe used to come to the East End regularly to have a drink with us, and we in turn, would go to the West End to see Joe, to return the compliment. He used to have his monogram on the left-hand side of the chest of his shirts, which were always beautiful linen.

The last time I saw Joe at the Astor Club, he proudly told me that that evening his baby son had been born, and he was going to call him Joe Junior. These twenty-five years later, Joe still visits, myself and Ron in Broadmoor. As you can guess, Joe is a loyal friend.

The Minder, Frank Kurylo

Winston's Club in the West End of London would be open until the early hours, and through the club doors would pass many celebrities, and different characters. An interesting person who would frequent the club regularly, was one Frank Kurylo, who was at one time the minder for Danny La Rue, and Joe Freeman, better known as Cockney Joe. Frank was one with handsome features despite the fact that he was one of the best knuckle fighters in the late fifties to seventies, and his attire was immaculate. Frank came from Leeds, so in a way it was quite unique how the London crowd took to him. This showed that he had a strong personality, the fact he was so accepted. Frank had taken over the job as minder for Danny La Rue when Billy Howard had relinquished his role. Frank was a good and loyal friend to Ron and I, and still is to the present day.

Big Pat Connelly

Big Pat, as he was known, had been on the firm for a number of years. As his name suggests, he was a Scotsman from Glasgow. We had first met Big Pat when we were on remand together at Brixton Prison. I had given Big Pat a job at the Double R Club as a part-time barman and doorman. Pat's weight was between seventeen and eighteen stone and he could punch his weight. He had a couple of scars on his face due to various battles he had been in, and when he and Limehouse Willy were fighting side by side, they were a good team to have on one's side. Limehouse Willy came from Bow Road, and was an ex-merchant seaman. He was a professional gambler, over six feet tall and was another member of the firm.

Sometimes old Dave Cohen would come into the Double R Club for a drink. He was one of the old tearaways of years ago. He had a bull neck and short cropped hair. He was an interesting character. Arthur Sutty was another friend who would visit the club. Billy Jones was given a three-year sentence when he was convicted of grievous bodily harm, along with Bobby Ramsey and my brother Ron, at the Old

Bailey. At one time Billy Jones had the Stragglers Club at Tower Court, Piccadilly, and Ron and myself were partners with him in this club. Billy had the nickname of 'The Fox' because he was so shrewd.

The Paddington Puncher

The reputation of Jimmy Smith spread beyond his area of Paddington to all parts of London. Jimmy was not a liberty-taker but a renowned fighting man, who would knock out adversaries, with just one or two punches. He was about five feet ten inches tall and had a powerful pair of shoulders. Paddington was an area known for its fighting men during the 1950s and 1960s, and Jimmy was part of the folklore spoken of in the Paddington vicinity and he was also a hard-drinking man.

When my brother Ron, and myself were in our early twenties, the names of people like Jimmy Smith, Nicky Carter and Jackie Rosa would crop up all the time. We found all these characters to be very colourful and fascinating. Each of these people were men of high calibre, and when I look back they all have a special memory as part of my past life, and I feel very fortunate to have been around at the same time as these interesting people. They all helped to make my past, and Ron's, that much more interesting.

I don't know if Jimmy is still alive, but if he is, I wish him happiness. The Paddington Puncher, Jimmy Smith is still talked about today. In his own way, he made his mark in life.

Billy Jones

Billy Jones was a regular at the Double R Club and most of the time we would talk about money-making schemes. Billy Donovan, who lived nearby the Double R Club, was another of the firm. He was an exceptionally good street fighter. Other fighting men who used the club were Les Burman, Arthur Sutty, Dougie King, Dave Simmons who was an ex-pro fighter, another ex-fighter Mossy Black, Joe Abrahams also an ex-pro fighter and Imie Rosen. Watney Street was known as a tough area, and the best in the area was Jimmy Fullerton. Jimmy was killed in a car crash at an early age.

Sometimes we would travel over to the area of Paddington, which also had its fighting men. Amongst these were Dave Barry, Billy Smith, and Nicky Carter. Dave Barry was a good money getter and club owner. At one time he hit a rival on the chin, and the fella never recovered consciousness. Dave was charged with manslaughter, he was convicted and given eighteen months in prison. In the Kings Cross area was Nicky Carlie. He had just come out of prison after doing seven years. He was a club owner and was always a happy-go-lucky character.

If we went to the Social Club in Clerkenwell, we would have a drink with Harry White, Micky Reagan and Jimmy Andrews. Finsbury Park was another good drinking area, and on this manor, Ruby Spanks, owner of the local pub 'The Favourite', could be found. He was an old-timer who had been in the Dartmoor mutiny many years ago. In the saloon bar would be Eddie and Jimmy Cardew, both ex-fighters, and their brothers, Charlie Clark, Freddie Andrews and Big Charlie Clark, the cat burglar from the area of Chingford.

If we took a stroll down Brick Lane on a Sunday morning, we might have come across old Arthur Hardy who sometimes used the name Harding. He had been a villain in his time and had been friends with my grandfather, Jimmy Kray. Old Arthur wrote a book about his experiences in the East End in later years.

On occasions we would drink in the Leicester Square area, and would go to a club owned by the shrewd Joe Wilkins. He was another who needed no minders. The London scene would not be complete without the mention of brothers Billy and Harry Heywood. They came from the Deptford area and Billy was sentenced to seven years for his part in the affray at Smiths Club in Catford. There had been a gun battle at this particular time at Smiths Club.

David Levy

David Levy was born in the area of Mile End, East London. He was one of a large Jewish family and was known as Davy Levy. Ron and I first met the Levy family when we were about seventeen years of age, and we became friends of the family.

Davy had a vicious temper, and all his family looked upon him as the leader in times of trouble. Davy had five brothers: Mossy, Joe, Bert, Sam and Artie. At one time Davy and myself had a row which led to both of us slinging punches at one another; in fact, when I slung the first punch at Davy, I knew he had concealed a knife up his sleeve by the way he had his arms crossed. Davy did use the knife, but I was lucky. The blade cut through the lapel on my suit and also through my waistcoat but it never reached my skin.

Sometime later we became friends again, and when Ron and myself were on the run from the Army, Davy and his family would let us stay in their little terrace home as long as we wanted.

Bert Rossi

Bert Rossi was convicted of the malicious wounding of Jack Spot, and was sentenced to four years in prison. Bert, better known as Battles Rossi, had been arrested for the attack on Jack Spot. During the time Bert was on remand during the attack charge, Ron and myself were also on remand in the same prison, Brixton, and we became friendly with Bert some years later. When we ran the Regency Club, Bert Rossi helped us in the gambling side of the club. He was one of the top gamblers in London during the fifties and sixties.

Tiny Bill

Tiny Bill was a well-known character and villain. He was about six feet six inches tall and of broad build. At one time he had entered a boxing competition for heavyweight, which was organized by the world famous boxing promoter, Jack Solomon. This was in the early 1950s. Tiny Bill, as he was known, won a couple of these fights before being beaten in the semi-finals. Tiny preferred fighting in the street rather than in the ring. At one time he had hit a fella so hard on the chin that he crashed his head onto the head of another person standing nearby, and as a result, the victim, and the one standing by were both knocked spark out. There were witnesses who saw this.

Tiny, at one time, was upset with some people who lived above the barber shop in Burnett Road, in the area of Mile End. Tiny blew all the windows out upstairs with a shotgun. Tiny himself also lived in the area of Mile End. His reputation spread throughout the East End of London, and in particular, through Chinatown, on the dockside area. Most people never did get to know his surname, and at the moment I cannot recall it, but I am sure that Tiny would be pleased to be remembered. At one time he used to be in the company of my brother Ron and I regularly and as one can imagine, he was an asset to the loosely knit firm, which was then in its early stages. Tiny died from cancer in his early fifties.

Patsy Manning

I first met Patsy Manning in 1957. I had just left the Regal Snooker Club to go to the stationery shop nearby when Patsy Manning stopped on the corner of

Eric Street, and said in his Brummie accent, 'Can you tell me where the nearest barber shop is mate?' I replied, 'Halfway down Burdett Road, you will find it on the left-hand side, it's Chris the Greek's shop. Tell him that I sent you. My name is Reg Kray and I am part-owner of the billiard hall just across the road there, and when you have finished your haircut, you can return here, and have a cup of tea with me in the billiard hall if you wish.' I noticed that Patsy was wearing a brown suit, and he had fierce blue eyes and there was a long scar down the right-hand side of his face which looked like a razor mark. Later, after we became friends, I found out from Patsy that he had in fact been scarred for life after a car crash.

Patsy had been a good friend to me and my family ever since that meeting. He was a villain but a likeable one who was born in Birmingham, sixty years ago as I write this story. Patsy and myself served time together in Long Lartin Prison when Patsy was serving a nine year sentence for malicious wounding, and I was serving my present life sentence. Patsy had been convicted after he had hit a fellow villain with a nine pound hammer, which caused the victim bad head injuries. Though Patsy could have had a fight, he had on this occasion used a hammer because the villain had ripped him off for a large sum of money which left Patsy skint.

Through the fifties and sixties, Patsy would visit our clubs whenever we had a gala night. One time I bet Patsy a fiver that he would not travel the world. Patsy did a world tour the rough way, so I lost my bet. He later wrote a book about his journeys which was published titled 'Crumpet All The Way'. He was very much a part of the fifties and sixties scene.

Arthur Thompson

On occasion Arthur Thompson would visit London to
see his contacts. For many years Arthur had control of
Glasgow. He was fearless, and was also feared by
many. Arthur had been blown-up at one time when
someone had planted a bomb in his car which went off
when he turned the ignition key. Although he survived
with serious injuries, his mother-in-law was killed in
the explosion. Arthur has also in the past been shot at,
and survived another time when someone attempted
to run him down with a speeding car.

Another Scotsman who we met was our friend
Jimmy Boyle. Jimmy came to the pub we had in
Cheshire Street, The Carpenters Arms. He was on the
run from the police at the time, and we arranged
accommodation for him. I found Jimmy to be a very
quiet person, and during his time at The Carpenters
Arms he only ever drank orange juice. Some years
later he served a life sentence for murder, and on his
release he has become a successful writer of books and
articles.

George and Alan Dixon

George and Alan Dixon were born in the area of
Poplar in East London. They are of the same age
group, and have always been close as brothers. When
Ron and I were convicted in 1969 the police, led by
detectives, concentrated their efforts on securing a

conviction against George and Alan Dixon, because the police said that the Dixons were trying to fill the void left by the Krays in East London.

The Dixons were convicted on the charge of demanding money from club owners, publicans and car dealers. George was seen to be the ringleader, and was given a twelve-year sentence, and Phil Jacobs who was convicted with them was also given twelve years.

George and Alan Dixon have been friends of my brother Ron and I for many years and I also knew Phil Jacobs. We first met George Dixon when he became a regular customer at the Regal Snooker Club just behind Mile End Road in East Road, East London. Ron and myself were owners of the Regal Snooker Hall between the years of 1957 and 1959. George Dixon was only about sixteen when he first became a member of the club.

He was a very tall kid with very powerful shoulders, and a very good-looking kid. Even at that early age, George was challenging and fighting men on a regular basis. George could have a fight and was confident of his capabilities as a fighter, and he and his brother Alan have always been likeable people. They both had a good sense of humour despite the fact that they were villains. I repeat 'were', because George and Alan are now happy in their present lifestyle. They told me this recently, when they came to visit me here at Blundestone Prison.

George, Alan and I had a laugh on their visit. We spoke of the time when I saved George's life, when he had ignored a request from Ron that he stay away from the Regency Gambling Club. This story has been told many times but I will repeat it nevertheless: Ron and myself, my brother Charlie and others were in the gambling club early one day. When George and some others entered the premises, I was sitting at the table with Ron. I was aware of Ron's request that George should stay away from the club. I noticed Ron's face change colour as George entered the gambling area, then Ron casually stood up and walked into the toilet which was a few feet away. I knew that Ron had a shooter hidden behind the cistern of the toilet and was sure that he had gone to the toilet to pick up the gun. As Ron came back from the toilet he pulled the gun out of his pocket and took aim at George Dixon who was close by. I acted very quickly and grabbed Ron's right hand which held the gun and pulled it towards the floor. There was a click from the hammer of the gun onto the bullet, so George was very lucky that he wasn't shot dead. At the same time as I grabbed the gun I shouted to George to fuck-off away from the place, and he and the others did so. Sometime later Ron gave George the particular bullet that had been meant for him. It had the indentation mark riveted on it.

Alan Dixon was also a good street fighter, and at times Alan and George would fight each other as furiously as they fought others. Both have marked faces from the many battles they were in during the fifties and early sixties, but George and Alan, both over six feet tall and of powerful build, are today smartly dressed and handsome men.

I recall that many years ago, when George was in the Rising Sun public house in Green Street, Bethnal Green, a fellow who disliked him, pulled a shotgun. However, before he could use it, George had smoothly and quickly pushed aside the gun and punched the fellow on the chin with a right-handed punch, knocking him to the floor where he lay spark out. This was all done in one movement. Another time, George upset some villains from North London, and they peppered his legs with a shotgun blast. George took it all in his stride, and was drinking in the clubs and pubs a couple of nights later. Yet another time George upset some South London people outside the Stork Club in Swallow Street, and the firm of South London people hit and kicked George from one end of the street to the other. He was still conscious and when the police questioned him as to who his attackers were, he told them to fuck-off.

To this day Alan and George have kept a good sense of humour. They recently told me that during the time of their prison sentence George had gone to see the prison governor and said to him: 'You have to get me out of this place, it is doing my head in. I can't eat this type of food you serve here for much longer, I'm used to good old East End pie and mash.'

Ron and Myself

When Ron and myself were eighteen years of age, we were on the run from the Army, and in our company was a man by the name of Paddy Austin, who lived in the Hoxton area. He too was on the run from the Army, and even though he was just eighteen years of age, he already had a reputation as a nutcase and a fighting man.

We would all sit about in Wally's Café, which was in London Fields at the back of Hackney. Ronnie Diamond who had what was known as 'The Diamond Gang' would also use the café. He was in the same age group as we were. Sometimes Ronnie Knight, who is now a resident of the Costa del Sol, would join us. At this time Ron Knight had an old taxi, and we would all clamber into the back and Ron would drive us all to the Royal Dance Hall in Tottenham where we would have a good night. Sometimes Ron Knight would invite us to his mother's flat to have supper. The flat was in the area of Dalston, and Ron's mother and the rest of her family were lovely people, as were Ron Knight himself and his brother Johnny.

Another one who used to use Wally's Café was Benny Robinson, whose brother committed a murder on a jeweller in a shop in Bethnal Green Road and who was hung for this murder. Benny Robinson would always be in the company of Kipper Hardy and the Bellamy family. All these people were fighting people and good money getters.

During the sixties all the firm would gather at The Lion pub in Tapp Street near Bethnal Green Junction, and sometimes we would decide to go and have a drink with our friend Freddie Foreman, at his pub just over London Bridge in Lant Street. The pub was the 'Prince of Wales', and we would all leave The Lion pub in Tapp Street, and would get into several cars and this convoy would arrive at Lant Street almost together. When we entered Fred's pub he would usually be there with his friend Ron Olives and a number of other friends, which would include the Hennessy brothers, and we would usually stay until closing time. Ron Olives and his brother Danny learnt to fight from their father who was an ex-fighter, and he had taught them well. The Hennessy brothers were also more than capable when it came to a row. Fred was always in full control of the pub and its company, and he was a good host.

We sometimes decided to go to the Latin Quarter Restaurant in Wardour Street for a supper and a drink. Paddy Onions from South London might be drinking at the bar. He was a respected person. Also in the bar might be Raymond Nash. He was a partner to Peter Rachman, who was the infamous rent collector.

King of the Con Men

One day Billy Hill phoned Ron and I, and said would we meet him at Pat Kennedy's pub, which was The Star in Belgravia Square, Knightsbridge. He wanted us to meet Charles Desilva.

I told Bill that we would be on our way. When we reached the public house, Bill ordered drinks for us, and introduced us to Charles Desilva. Bill told us that Charlie Mitchell had been taking liberties with Charles Desilva, by blagging money off him, and he also said that Desilva would prefer to pay Ron and me money regularly rather than let Mitchell blag him, so would we mind him. Ron and I agreed to do so, and shook hands with Charles to bind our agreement. We drank and talked with Bill and Charles for about an hour, and then left the pub, but not before we had agreed to meet Charles the following day at one of London's best hotels, where Charles had a full suite. He always lived in style, and was booked into the hotel as a sheikh.

Charles was born in Indonesia, and had a tanned complexion, jet black hair, perfect white teeth, and good looks in general. He wore just enough jewellery and was a perfect dresser. Charles was known in criminal circles as 'The King of the Con Men', and when he conned someone, it was always for enormous amounts of money.

When Ron and I met him at the hotel, he gave us a considerable sum of money, which would be a regular income for looking after him. Charles came from a wealthy family and was used to high living, and he had impeccable manners. He told us that he could have been wealthy by working in the confines of his family's business, but preferred the excitement and buzz of pulling off a big con. He would drive a Rolls Royce or a Bentley and would only dine in the most exclusive hotels, clubs or restaurants.

Sometime later he was arrested on a fraud charge and gaining money by deception, and was given a seven-year sentence which he spent mainly at Parkhurst Jail. Prison life had a bad effect on Charles, because it was alien to his style of living, and the insensitivity of the majority of the inmates was not good for his frame of mind. When he got out of prison he said he would not return, but he resumed in his position as the top con man.

A little while later Charles was arrested for selling a fleet of yachts to a couple of farmers, which were sold for somewhere in the region of one million pounds. The yachts were non-existent. Charles was given bail and sent for trial. While awaiting trial, he continued to enjoy his luxurious lifestyle, but one night just before the commencement of his trial he went to an exclusive hotel, booked a suite of rooms, ordered a bottle of the best champagne, and took an overdose of tablets with a glass of champagne and never recovered consciousness. Charles left a suicide note saying that he could

100

not face another term in prison and would his family forgive him, hence his suicide.

I would always remember Charles Desilva, who had the looks of Omar Sharif and bearing the style of a sheikh. He will always remain in my mind as the King of the Con Men, who it was our pleasure to meet.

Carmelo Messina

In the year 1959, I had just been sentenced to eighteen months in prison for demanding money with menaces, despite the fact that I was innocent. I was sitting on a wooden bench below the court of the Old Bailey when the screws opened the cell door to admit another who had just been convicted in the court above. As he entered he introduced himself to me. He was Carmelo Messina who was one of the infamous Messina brothers.

He was short in height and had swarthy dark skin and was very polite. His birthplace was Malta, and Carmelo and his brothers were infamous for running a call-girl racket in central London during the early 1950s until the 1960s.

The family were multi-millionaires due to the vice racket they ran. Carmelo told me that on his conviction he was innocent, and the police from West End Central Police Station had convinced a prostitute to give false evidence against him, that she paid Carmelo from immoral earnings from selling herself on the streets. For this Carmelo had been sentenced to four years' imprisonment. I found Messina an interesting person, and when we both arrived at Wandsworth Prison to start our sentence I asked a few people to watch out for Carmelo, because though I disliked ponces, I looked upon Carmelo in a different light, because as he told me, and others told me the same, that to live off a woman in the country of Malta was not considered immoral, and whichever way one looked upon the Messina family, they were professional in the particular field they chose as a means of living.

Many years later around about the year 1967, Ron and myself received a message from Carmelo Messina, that if we would travel to Malta to see him and his family, he had a proposition to put to us. This showed that he had not forgotten my presence during the dreary days at Wandsworth Prison.

Ron and I never made this trip to Malta because sometime later we were arrested which led to my present residence. The Messina name has a place in the annals of professional crime, and a place in my memory of the colourful 1950s and 1960s, and today I still wonder what proposition Carmelo and his family had in mind.

The Don of Dons

One evening in 1966, I had a meet with some Americans in the Pigalle Restaurant Club in Regent Street. The meeting was to be in the bar of the club. When I got there, there were four Americans present, two of them I knew and the other two were strangers. These people were men of respect, and I will never forget this particular night, because in the small group one of them was about seventy years of age. He was a small-built man and had dark skin, he was clearly of Sicilian heritage, and it was pretty obvious that his three friends held him in reverence. At one stage of the conversation someone passed the cigarettes around, and I lit my lighter for one of these friends who was to my left. As I did so he said to me in a friendly tone of voice, 'Reg, would you light the cigarette of our friend here first out of respect, because he is the elder,' and the friend on my left gestured with his hand to the Sicilian-looking man on my right. This was a lesson in respect I shall never forget.

The names of these men will remain unsaid. Throughout the night I learned that the elder man who was held in reverence was a Don of Dons.

Men of Respect

Some of these men of respect were fascinating storytellers about people, and also about their own experiences. One of these I used to meet in a London hotel. His first name was Herb. I will keep his surname to myself. We would sit and have a coffee while he told me fascinating stories. Sometimes I would get to the hotel early to join him for breakfast, and he would sit at the table wearing an immaculate white satin dressing gown of short length.

One of the nicest people it has been my pleasure to meet, was a man of respect whose first name was Joe. His city was Washington DC. He was a classy dresser, he was very mild-mannered and wore smart tinted glasses. His fingernails were manicured to perfection and he wore just enough jewellery of class without being ostentatious. Charlie, Ron and myself would meet Joe and his charming wife at the Hilton Hotel on regular occasions. Joe had come up through the ranks, and was now recognized as a top man of the family. At one time in his younger days, Joe had been convicted of knifing a man to death during a backstreet dice game.

Joe used to go to the island of Antigua on holiday and on business trips, and he invited me on a trip with him. All these years later I regret that I did not join him on the trip, but often life does not work out the way we would like it to. Looking back, Joe was one of my favourite people.

Charlie White, alias 'The Blade', used to phone Ron from the island of Antigua. Ron used to find top croupiers for Charlie White and put them in touch with him to help him in his organized gambling. Charlie White was a big man as far as respect is concerned. I say was because he passed away in the late seventies.

There was amongst these people one by the name of 'Skinny' who lived in an old precinct building in New York. Others told me that although he was very frail in build he really used to put the fear into people. At one time there was a world heavyweight fight champion who had not done what he was told for Skinny and his friends, so Skinny met his champ and invited him for a talk in Skinny's car. He drove round a few blocks while talking to the heavyweight, and it was said that at the end of the drive the heavyweight was shaking so bad through fear that when he got out of the car he could hardly stand. I point out this particular story to show that men of violence are of all shapes and sizes, and are not necessarily big men, physically.

A Man Amongst Men

Little Joe was from New York and when he passed away recently all the men of respect were genuine in the sadness they felt. Joe was considered 'The Man Amongst Men' and all had and showed respect for him. Little Joe, like many of his friends and associates had known what it was like to be without a cent, and had risen through the ranks of the concrete jungle to be a man of respect and wealth. He always remembered his days of hunger and would give precious gifts freely to his friends. Just a few years ago, my brother Ron received a beautiful gold ring with diamonds, which Joe had sent to Ron at Broadmoor all the way from New York.

Joe and Ron had been friends for a number of years, and distance did not make their friendship any the less. They had exchanged cards on occasions and particularly at Christmas. When Joe passed away Ron was very upset and he wrote a poem dedicated to Joe, which Ron sent to Joe's family in tribute.

Sicilian Eddie

Eddie the Sicilian was a man of respect, and I leave out his surname for the sake of his family and for other obvious reasons. Eddie visited London in the mid sixties, and during this time Charlie, Ron and myself made him welcome as our guest. Eddie was about five feet ten-and-a-half inches tall and his shoulders were as powerful and broad as any I had seen. He came from New York, had Sicilian blood, but he had contacts all over the world, which included gambling, show business and fight contacts. Eddie stayed at one of the main hotels in London, and we would meet him in his room before taking him on a tour of London and for late drinking sessions at 'The Society' in Germain Street, just at the back of Regent Street. I recall that the first time we met him, in the room at his hotel, there was a large radiogram in his room and Eddie switched it on, so that the music could be heard. He said he did this so the music would drown any conversation if the room was bugged.

We would drink with Eddie and some of his friends in The Society until the early hours of the morning. Eddie would drink glasses of scotch and water, and we joined him in this particular drink, and he was surprised and said so, that me and my brothers never got drunk. He would tell us fascinating stories of celebrities, and the top people who lived in the States. Eddie invited me to go and visit his family in Sicily with him. I took this to be the ultimate in respect being shown to me. I regret to say, due to circumstances at the time, I never did get to accept the invitation to meet Eddie's family in Sicily. Eddie was only in his mid forties when he was shot dead by two hitmen somewhere in New York.

Angelo Bruno

When Angelo Bruno, the late Philadelphia boss came to London, Ron and myself were invited to meet him. We first met him at the Hilton Hotel. Angelo was very short in height and had a stocky build. At the time of the meeting he wore a beret, which covered his bald head, and he wore glasses. We had a cup of coffee with him and he asked questions about London centred around gambling clubs.

He was looking for premises in London and so the three of us hailed a taxi, and I instructed the driver to take us to Knightsbridge where I showed Angelo some premises. We also showed him premises in the Tottenham Court Road area, but this never came to anything.

Ron and myself met Angelo another couple of times. Once was in a little restaurant in the Soho area. Another time we had a drink with him in the Winter Gardens Hotel, Knightsbridge.

Angelo told us that if anyone upset his people he

would say to them, 'If you kick the dog, you kick the master,' and he said this with menace in his tone of voice, to any that upset his friends or those he was in business with.

Years later Angelo Bruno was shot dead; he was riddled with bullets when he was sitting in his car in his own town of Philadelphia.

Tony Ducks Carrello

Tony Ducks Carrello is now serving a sentence for one hundred years in a jail somewhere in America. He was convicted of extortion and other charges. Tony Carrello was born in Brooklyn, New York, and was a main man in the garment industry. Sometimes during the mid fifties, Tony Ducks Carrello came to London and stayed in a flat in the Bayswater area. He had a friend with him who also came from Brooklyn. Tony and his friend had invited Charlie, Ron and myself to join them at the flat so we could talk on things in general which revolved around London. They had also invited Tony Mulla to join them, but Tony did not show up. Tony and his friend were not happy with Mulla for his lack of respect and they mentioned this. I recall during the conversation, Tony's friend opened with a tin-opener cans of Libby's tomato juice and passed them to Tony and ourselves. Tony invited us to go and see him and be his guests in Brooklyn whenever we wanted to, and he would show us around New York. Much to my regret, we did not make the journey, though Ron did go to New York years later, of which I will tell. Tony was short and very thickset, had a broken nose and had a strong Brooklyn accent. Tony and his friend came across as good people, but at the same time, not people to mess with.

Tony Punchie Illiano

Punchie Illiano was an ex-fighter at middleweight. He had turned professional at an early age and was reasonably successful. Since his fighting days he had become a man of respect and was also a New York nightclub owner. Ron met Tony Illiano when he went to New York and they got on well together. Tony had taken Ron to his club, and had shown him around the other nightspots in New York. In the 1960s there was a connected family in Brooklyn, New York, who had become infamous over the years, and were portrayed as the gangsters of that era. They were the Gallo family, led by Crazy Joe Gallo and his brothers, Larry and Al. Crazy Joe had become a legend because of his wild exploits and behaviour. He kept a tiger in a cage in the basement of the house he lived in and if he was upset with anyone he would show him the caged tiger and would threaten to chuck them in the cage with the animal.

At one time Crazy Joe heard that Billy Daniels, the coloured singer who had made famous the song 'That Old Black Magic', had been dating one of Joe's girlfriends who was a good-looking air hostess. He had taken Billy to see the ferocious tiger, and it was said that forever after Billy Daniels never looked at an air hostess again, other than to order a quick gin and tonic. Crazy Joe had also been kicked out of the Army, having been classified as a psychopath.

Larry and Al Gallo were also more capable when it came to handling problems and people, but were considered mild in comparison with their brother Joe. Crazy Joe was eventually shot dead while dining in a restaurant in the area of Little Italy in New York, but he had managed to follow the three hitmen as far as the pavement outside the restaurant before he collapsed and died in the gutter. This was considered to be the classic gangland killing and once again the name of Crazy Joe Gallo hit headlines across the newspapers of the day.

When Ron first went to New York, he and Joe Kaufman, went to a small café situated in the Little Italy area. Outside the café they were met by Edmondo, who was a little dwarf, and was mascot to the Gallo family and to their friend, Tony Punchie Illiano. My brother Ron, who had no fear of people or situations, had gone to the café to seek out and to introduce himself to Crazy Joe Gallo and his brothers. Edmondo showed Ron and Joe Kaufman into the café and asked them to sit down at the table and wait while he went into the kitchen area of the café to make a phonecall.

A few minutes later a group of people were encircled around Ron and Joe Kaufman, and one of these was Punchie Illiano, who asked Ron and Joe a few questions so that he could check them out on credibility of who they were. Eventually after Punchie had checked them out, Al Gallo arrived on the scene and met Ron and Joe. Ron was told that Crazy Joe was not available, he was away on business and Larry Gallo was in hospital dying of cancer. Ron arranged, as a sign of respect, to send Larry a basket of fruit.

During conversation with Tony Illiano at his club Ron said to Tony 'Exactly how many of the Gallo brothers are there?' and Tony replied, 'There are Joe, Larry, Al and myself.' This was Tony's way of saying that he was part of the family.

Ron made plans for Tony to be our guest in London, but this never came about because a little while after this Ron and I were sentenced to life imprisonment.

Al Gallo is still alive and books have been written on Crazy Joe Gallo, and a film was also made about them. A few years ago I read a *Sunday Times* magazine, and there was an article and photographs of Tony Illiano and his friends. It showed he was a good dresser just as Ron said. Tony had fair hair, blue eyes, a broken nose and was well-built. I would imagine he sees Al and himself as the only two left of the Gallo family. That's loyalty.

Charlie Kray

My brother Charlie had twenty-two professional fights and yet when the firm was strong I never knew of him taking any liberties with anyone. In fact he would rather help someone than do them harm. That is why he is still respected all over the country today.

111

Ron Kray alias The Colonel

Ron is a very complex character, often contradictory, sometimes eccentric. I've known him to be vicious when necessary but deep down he has a very kind nature. Anyone who has met Ron will confirm that he is immaculate in his dress sense and is always a perfect gentleman. One time Ron and I were in the Greengate public house and Ron was sitting on a bar stool, three fellas entered the bar and stood directly behind Ron making sarcastic remarks against him. I was watching and listening to all of this but before I could make a move, Ron beat me to it. He stepped down off the stool and hit the fella on the left with a right-handed punch and he went down immediately like a windless bagpipe. Ron then turned his body and shoulders and hit his friend on the right with a beautiful left hook, leaving him also to be picked off the floor. The third joker looked on in amazement, his face went ashen then he apologized profusely to Ron and made for the exit.

Ron was completely fearless and one incident I recall when this trait stood out, involves his meeting with the Maltese. One particular day either four or five Maltese from the Commercial Road pulled up outside the billiard hall in Eric Street. Two of them entered the hall and had the audacity to demand money off Ron. Ron didn't hesitate, he picked up a large sword which he kept behind the bar and chased the Maltese out of the hall and back to their car with the sword, smashing the windows and causing as much damage as he possibly could before the ignition fired and they sped away to safety.

Ron is a very philanthropic man as anyone who

knows him will verify. When we were in Tangier, he unofficially adopted an Arab in the Casbah by the name of Larby. Larby had been a very intelligent person at one time but had been imprisoned as a political prisoner and was ruthlessly tortured. When he regained his freedom he had little choice but to survive by begging. Ron gave him suits and other attire and looked after him in general, enabling Larby to regain his dignity.

Ron also has a good sense of humour. When we were in Nigeria on business, he was asked if he wished to visit any particular place and Ron said he did, the local prison, as he was very interested in criminology. His wish was granted and Ron toured the prison as an important dignitary.

Ron is a very humble person and has deep humility. He was certified insane during his sentence and sent to Broadmoor where he has been for ten years. Ron has held the hand of both the brother and sister of life, joy and sorrow. Now it is the time for him to reflect occasionally back to the past, to enjoy the present, yet still retain hope for the future. He is the most loyal of friends, even if at times he has been known to be a bad enemy. I hope that in his twilight years it will be taken into consideration that he has responded well to treatment during his time at Broadmoor. In the decade which he's spent there, he has been a model patient and I hope and pray he will be considered for release, so that he can spend the remainder of his life peacefully.

Reg Kray

I hesitate to talk about myself in great length for fear that it may seem egotistical and that I condone violence as a way of life but I feel that I should mention myself in a factual manner or else it could be said that I fear to do so. These writings it might be said, will remain incomplete unless I do speak about myself, on the debit side or credit side, depending on which way one looks at the nature of the story.

I have shot four people in the past, missed two others. On the physical side, I was like Ron and I stress the word, was. I could punch hard with either hand, so much so that I broke eleven jaws, that I know of. I would also like to stress that without excuse but as fact, that like Ron I was a product of my environment. I regarded myself as a club owner and believe myself to have been a good host as I enjoyed the work and ambience of our establishments. To be truthful, I was in my element making people happy rather than creating misery. Like Ron, I too am in my twilight years and I also look forward to the day when I can take my first steps to freedom to spend the rest of my life in peace. I hope that my writings show that it is better to read such stories from the comfort of an armchair than to participate in such criminal activities. I hope the same writings will be considered as a social document of some value and I will be remembered as much for being an author, as I have for being a villain.

Since this book went to print Mr Geoff Allen passed away on 25 December 1992. Geoff, who is one of the characters in this book, which the Twins looked upon as an Uncle, was a very dear friend and will be sadly missed.

He bought a shop in Town Street, Thaxstead, and converted it into a restaurant which he named 'The Blind Beggar', in honour of his friends, the Twins.

When the restaurant was completed he hung a large swinging sign outside; it was a replica of the sign outside The Blind Beggar pub in the East End.

1975 A sign of friendship with the Kray twins.